THE
TROUBLE
WITH
DAYDREAMS

THE TROUBLE WITH DAYDREAMS

COLLECTED & NEW POEMS

MARK VINZ

Legacy Series
Volume 2

NDSU NORTH DAKOTA STATE
UNIVERSITY PRESS

Fargo, North Dakota

NDSU NORTH DAKOTA STATE UNIVERSITY PRESS

NDSU Dept. 2360, P.O. Box 6050
Fargo, ND 58108-6050
www.ndsupress.org

The Trouble with Daydreams: Collected and New Poems, by Mark Vinz

Legacy Series Volume 2 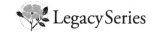 Legacy Series

First Edition

David Bertolini, Director
Suzanne Kelley, Publisher
Oliver West Sime, Graduate Assistant in Publishing
Kyle Vanderburg, Publishing Intern

Cover illustration and design by Jamie Trosen
Interior design by Deb Tanner

The publication of *The Trouble with Daydreams: Collected and New Poems* is made possible by the generous support of the Muriel and Joseph Richardson Fund and donors to the NDSU Press Fund and the NDSU Press Endowed Fund.

ISBN: 978-1-946163-41-7
LCCN: 2021942166

Printed in the United States of America

This paper meets the requirements of ANSI/NISO Z39.48-1992 (Permanence of Paper).

for Betsy, who showed me the way

for Katie and Sarah, who taught me what it meant

"By the close study of a place, its people and character, its crops, products, paranoias, dialects, and failures, we come closer to our reality . . . Location, whether it is to abandon it or draw it sharply, is where we start."

—*Louise Erdrich*

"Love, children, and work. All the rest is incidental."

—*Paul Gruchow*

CONTENTS

From *Minnesota Gothic* and *Affinities*

From *Long Distance* and *The Work Is All*

From *In Harm's Way* and *Permanent Record*

New and Uncollected Poems

PREFACE

Fifty years of writing poems and teaching poetry and poetry writing have led to many hard choices when it comes to making selections for a volume such as this one, especially given all the people and memories attached to each piece.

I must begin with the two men I consider both inspirations and mentors, without whose help I wouldn't have gotten very far: Thomas McGrath, world class poet and tutor, who gave me my first real lessons as a writer and was the main reason I founded and edited the poetry magazine *Dacotah Territory* magazine and press, and Roland Dille, who made possible so many projects during his years as president of Moorhead State University, a man who supported poets as much as academics, as in his suggestions to give grants to the magazine and press and to establish a visiting writers series.

Many of us work best in a community of writers and friends who give advice and encouragement. From my first months in Fargo-Moorhead, Tony Oldknow stands out as a kind of dynamo, editing books and magazines as well as producing his own work and organizing readings, which at first were judged successful if the audience outnumbered the writers. And Joe Richardson, who has become my closest friend and who has taught me more than anyone, especially working with him in the founding and operation of Plains Distribution Service, with its traveling Bookbus, which, while it lasted during the 1970s, became nationally known as a distributor of midwestern small press publications.

In the early 1980s, after Tom McGrath had retired and Plains Distribution had shut down, Thom Tammaro became a colleague, good friend, co-editor of several anthologies, and co-director of the visiting writers series. And Jim White, who, up to his untimely death in 1985 loved to "talk poems" and expanded my horizons in ways no other has. There were many

Writers in the Schools friends as well: Molly La Berge, George Roberts, and Dave Solheim chief among them, and editors such as Bill Truesdale, David Pichaske, Tom Montag, Ted Kooser, Orv Lund, John Judson, Paul Janeczko, E.V. Griffith, Robert Alexander, and Scott King. And in his role as Literature Program Director of the National Endowment for the Arts, no one did more to support and encourage small press and literary magazines than another friend, Leonard Randolph. Finally, Greg Danz, bookstore owner and sponsor of many readings. How I admire those who have labored in the fields of "non-commercial" literature! There are many others whom I remember and feel gratitude for knowing, but I especially need to mention Tom Hansen, my friend and pen pal, who's provided insights and editorial suggestions I've come to rely on. Given my life among people such as these, the terms *labor of love* and *thankful* are the ones I've used more than any others. All praises to my fellow writers and to those who read and otherwise support our work!

Finally, while choosing poems for this collection I've tried to make representative selections that show my varying emphases over the years as well as my development as a writer.

Mark Vinz

FIRST PUBLISHED
IN CHAPBOOKS,
1975–1980

Ritual

Old men are dancing tonight in Fargo,
and in a hundred towns in Minnesota
Viking bands are braying polkas to the
      Northern Cross.
Accordions seduce fat women in corners.
Naked clarinets prance and twist behind
      a gauze of smoke.

Children, where are your parents tonight?
The doors to their mead halls are locked
and the darkness grows heavy
with the ceremony of their secret singing.

At the Battle Monument

There are few signs of the enemy now—
no one marked his passing on that day.
Tourists wander beside fences
dreaming out their own imperfect histories, alone—
all these lost children
locked forever in each other's arms.

But when the morning struck their eyelids
for that last long time
how they must have wondered:
their God, their battle song,
the precious country they wore on their backs
like a robe of light.

In the distance, they marked
the soldiers where they fell:
an army of white stones
                      camped on the hillsides,
where there will soon be darkness
invading the houses of the prairie grass,
where so many have been drowned
in their own sweet blood.

Valley of the Kaw

They lived here once, in this valley,
where the moon hangs in the river
like the pocket watch of a president,
where smoke from a factory
festers like smallpox.

A warrior night hawk
shrieks out his last circle
and drops back into dark.

River, trees and speechless ground—
they called themselves
The Children of the Wind.
Who will call our names
when we are gone?

Gladys and Alma

No one remembers just how long
They've lived in their museum
of clocks and calendars,
afghans, vases, coffee cups.

Today they voyage out
as far as the corner,
surveying the sidewalks
like anxious squirrels.
It's difficult to tell
which one is in the lead
or holds the other up.

My friends, who is to say
these mute uncharted faces
are not our final blessings?
Who is to know this tiny
piece of sky that shelters us
does not rest solely on their
beautiful and crooked backs?

Red River Blues

Tonight the news of drought
sweeps in on western winds—
topsoil laced with smoke and snow.
Nothing can stop that message here.

The empty rain gauge chants
the last faint summer dreams;
around the house the earth
has sunk another inch this week.

Even flat land falls away: this is
the place where all directions cease.
Just past town is the only hill—
the overpass for the interstate.

November Song

Tonight, the first snow,
the starless dark we
wrap our coats around,
clinging to autumn
like the last dry leaf.

The wind is a stalker
rattling all our doors,
the wind is a beggar
wanting only to be loved.

A long fast freight
tunnels through town—
Montana coal train
riding its black message
from the west,
ringed in frost and smoke.
In each small fire
there is a tiny song of sleep.

Tonight, the first snow dreams—

the wind is an old beggar
rattling our bones in his cup.

Driving Through

This could be the town I'm from,
marked only by what it's near.
The gas station man speaks of weather
and the high school football team
just as I knew he would—
kind to strangers, happy to live here.

I tell myself it doesn't matter now,
I'm only driving through.
Past the sagging, empty porches
locked up tight to travelers' stares,
toward the great dark of the fields,
my headlights startle a flock of
old love letters—still undelivered,
en route for years.

Line Storm

for Gene Frumkin

Only the wind is moving now, the grass
    turning in upon itself.
The farmer's boots stand empty on the porch.
Even the windows sleep.

Suddenly the eyes of the clouds are open,
the lightning stalks the windrows five miles down,
    closer and closer . . .

Out in the fields, all the
abandoned machines begin to awaken—
corn pickers, combines, balers
circling in a heavy dance,
rooting the ground with their snouts.
An ancient John Deere tractor is leading them . . .
westward, toward the conspiracy of clouds
    the iron voices of the lightning.

And now they are waiting:
steaming and shuddering in the first assault of rain.

Winter Promises

The funeral procession
creeps out from behind the church,
a long black snake filled with
the faces of captive children
and fingers drawing backward
messages on the steamed glass.

But what do they do with the bodies
when it's 15 below,
when the ground's as hard
as this ice-ridden road,
deep down
deeper than any grave
impossible to dig?

I dream of them
stacked like cordwood
in some refrigerated vault,
waiting for spring thaw,
the mansions of heaven
temporarily delayed.

I dream of them
in the dark cellars of the prairie,
frozen with the potatoes,
with rocks and tent poles,
broken pots and buffalo meat.

And here above ground:
the frosty halos of our breath,
the driven snow
that flies in through our eyes.

From *Letters to the Poetry Editor*

I. *Dear Sir,*

I am a confessional poet
from Decatur, Illinois.
My mother is a librarian,
my father sells used cars.
My poems, as you will see
are mostly about snakes
and sunsets.

After all,
how much is there to confess
in Decatur, Illinois?

II. *to whom it may concern:*

No one knows how a poet suffers.
These are some of my poems.
They are about suffering.
I have collected nearly 3,000
rejection slips in the last 5 years.

Please send me one of yours.

IV. *Dear Shithead:*

This makes 14 poems y've
rejected this spring alone.
The shit you print reflects
yr taste. It's eds. like
yrself who ruin it all &
I just hope yr pleased.

(p.s. enclosed find
five new poems)

VI. *Ed.:*

I have published nearly 100 poems
in the third quarter of this year,
in magazines too numerous
to mention here.

Enclosed find 20 poems to consider.

If you recognize my name
(and you should)
I'm sure you'll give my poems
the close attention they deserve.

IX. *Editor:*

Over a week ago, I sent you
15 poems. As yet I have not
received a reply.
Kindly take what you like
and send the rest directly on
to Denver Quarterly.

It's already August, and I'm
still not through the D's.

XI. *Dear Editor,*

This is the greatest poem
I have written thus far.
I'm told that when poets
complete a work they appear
in some kind of literary magazine.

I am now ready to appear.

XIV. *Dear Editor,*

Even though I've never been
west of the Hudson River,
I feel a strong kinship for
the Great Plains. There are
barns & blizzards in these
poems, & lots of Indians.
Do you see many of these
where you are?

XXI. *My friend:*

I am an ethnic poet. Here are 42 Chicano
poems, all written during my visit to El
Paso last month. Should you not find these
interesting, I will be happy to send you
more work. Please indicate your preferences,
according to the following list:

American Indian (specify tribe)
Black (specify degree of militancy)
Eskimo
New England fisherman
Midwestern farmer (specify crop)
Southwestern Adobe

P.S. My first book of poems will be
available soon. It's called *Twenty
Aztec Verses and a Leaping
Scandinavian Quartet*

FROM
CLIMBING THE STAIRS

Sleepless, Reading Machado

I.

Beneath the desk lamp
these small songs,
a sea wind bearing
tiny yellow flowers,
a sleeper moaning
in another room.

II.

Consider for this moment
the joy of solitude,
the grief of empty rooms.

So little changes:
not the ship, or the storm,
or the eternal hunger of
the waves. Only the faces,
the fear of going down.

III.

And this:
new snow in the night
covering the fresh
spring grass. Bird
tracks wandering alone
in the moonlight.

Some call it sorrow,
some call it love.

IV.

Toward morning
the words grow darker
against the page.
Darker and longer
beside the clock radio
humming to itself on a table,
and the wind
just moving the curtains.

Someone whistles
beneath the window,
and footsteps walk away—
my own song returning
as the first light
gathers in the trees.

Business as Usual

Under the dining room light
the old conspiracy flickers:
who failed the checkbook this time,
who hid the newspaper, spilled the soda,
left windows open in the rain . . .?

The children are upstairs in bed
listening to the grass growing—
it's simple now, in moonlight.
All day they have been speaking to
Mr. South Wind, asking favors:
blow away the neighbors
in their lawn chairs, bring
some new friends in a balloon.

But fathers are useful, too.
I'm required to teach them how to spell
so they can write their dreams,
required to learn a magic chant
to make tornadoes go away,
and watch their hands, and sing.

And since I cannot fix the TV set
or the ugly eye of a ceiling leak,
cannot make the insects stop
squashing themselves against the screens,
since I am not on speaking terms with
the south wind, or the cupboard crickets,
or even the column of figures
I helped to invent,

it's really the least I can do

here beside the window
and a whole army of healthy grass
growing greener
growing loud
in the last lovely light
of the moon, the moon, the moon.

Midcontinent

for Dave Williamson, Beyond Borders

Something holds us here—
call it the madness of phone lines,
the pride of blizzards,
the love of wheels and wind.

Something holds us here,
where roads don't ever seem to end.
Our maps are letters home
we don't know where to send.

In a Drought Year

for Joe

The barn was empty,
falling down,
the windmill bent
like a discarded paper hat.
We passed a hundred like it—
talked of mountains, surf,
anything to keep us from
the heat and dying corn—
until we stopped
to watch an orange moon rise
and string our breaths
across those cooling fields—
going nowhere,
but going home.

A Harvest

It is autumn, when the geese
chime midnight just above your roof,
when you remember nearly everything
you couldn't live without all these years—
perhaps what keeps you sleepless
on the nights you'd least expect
betrayal from your oldest friends—
the moon, a few certain stars and sounds,
shadows from the elm trees
just inside the deepest dark.

Tonight is autumn and the geese have gone.
God, like some grandfather who has died too soon,
perhaps is laughing softly now
at all your metaphors—
just as you laugh your tiredest, shuddering self
backward through the lengthening nights.
But the child upon the stairs is sleepless too,
wakened by a speeding car with music
that some nerve inside you hates.
Together you will listen to the leaves—
whatever drops away, whatever stays.

Quilt Song
for Alec Bond

A mist of snowflakes swirling in the street—
another blizzard? You've lost all track.
Astonished April waits somewhere
beyond the trees: not this week, not yet,
we'll test you for a few more days,
let your temper stretch itself another notch,
then give you floods—
just in case you thought you deserved better.

One more time you unfold the
old grandmother's quilt,
the one she called the Double Wedding Ring.
The child you once were used it
as a racetrack for tiny cars,
a kingdom home from school,
a comforter against most chills
and winds that still find all the cracks.

You walk the pattern one more time:
what you find is lost, and what
is lost remains, like an unfinished winter.
Warmed again, you wait
while snowflakes swirl in golden double loops.

North Dakota Gothic

The farm was abandoned
nearly three months ago.
Someone has stolen the mailbox,
the roofless house still reeks of smoke.

Beside the road,
a field of sunflowers
leans against the frost
like some forgotten army,
heads down and waiting.

Across a bare elm branch
the wind brings news of early snow.

From the Dream Journal

1. Charter Line

At the first sign of
weariness, there will be
a fifteen-minute rest stop.
The company has assured
us this is true.

The driver wears sunglasses
and a leather vest.
He never turns around.

No one thinks to ask
if we are behind schedule,
or why outside the windows
trees and wildflowers
are turning black.
No one consults a map.

After the first twenty-four hours
the road begins to
disappear. This doesn't
seem to worry the passengers.
All tickets have been
paid for in advance.

2. Junta

Someone is sleeping in the back row.
It is Friday—class is never good on Friday,
but we are here because the liberal arts demand it,
because we have a need to continue.

Eyeballs roll back and forth
in the chalk trays, clicking.
The clock leaps through the window.
A dictionary is chewing my left leg.

The class is mildly amused.

Three colonels in the back row
grin through hair and football helmets.
A girl in a cheerleader suit stands
and identifies herself as a CIA agent.

    The poet, ten years old, is ripping
    covers off textbooks in the back row.

The bell will not ring—they have stolen the bell!
They have stolen the pens and paper and chalk!
In the corner, my grandmother nods
and looks up from her knitting.

    The poet, fourteen years old, is gouging
    someone else's initials on a desk.

Motorcycles cruise the corridors.
Sledgehammers creep out from book bags.
Someone pours kerosene on the desk.

The poet, eighteen years old,
dozes in the back row.

I try to pinch my arm, but my
fingers have turned into paper clips.

Grandma smiles and cocks her rifle.

3. Discount Shopping
      for Jim Stevens

We never see each other
outside these barn-like walls—
the fat Madonnas cradling
babies, blouses, plastic boots,
the husbands wheeling loads of
tires and motor oil.
Today the uniform is bulging
orlon tops and papery double-knits.
A herd of pimples rummages
the 8-track tapes, old campaigners
form a skirmish line of canes,
checkout artists pop their gum at 90 rpm.
Ever wonder why the faces never change?

Beneath this store and parking lot
a secret city sprawls—
it's where the workers go after hours
to reproduce the merchandise
and engineer the sales.
Most of the shoppers live there too—
study muzak, elbowing, and cartsmanship—
come up to browse on eight-hour shifts.

Now and then a few defect:
they disappear for weeks, then overnight
put up bungalows at the edge of town.

4. A Dream of Fish

Childhood is that place you visit often now,
each year a few more parts of it called back
like fish rising toward the surface of a lake,
darting closer and closer
to your hand in the water.

There is a fish called Grandmother
and a fish called Summer Camp.
There are fish with only savage teeth and eyes,
and you too are a fish, or several,
shadowy and distorted in the green light.

Deep down other shapes are moving—
you can only guess what they look like
and wonder if they too will rise
to your outstretched fingers,
if they too will elude your grasp.

FROM
MIXED BLESSINGS

From a *North County Journal*
Mary Graham Vinz (1882–1972)

I.

As if by instinct now
the car tracks eastward through
the flat Red River Valley land
toward frozen lakes and hills.
The towns are copies of each other here,
squatting listlessly among their monuments
against the edges of the fields:
water tower, elevator, gas station,
bar, railroad semaphore, church . . .

We have been taught
that when the ones we love are dying
we must go.
The slow deaths are the worst,
most like our own.

Nothing moves except the road.

II.

She talks of death as I talk of life,
half believing, each of us an emissary
watching the other's eyes.
I hold her hand and read aloud
the letters from old friends,
filled with their own dying.
The heart machine ticks onward, implacably,
its message and her own the same:
one day is no different from the rest.

III.

Once there were glaciers here.
Now only winter, and the terrible
survivor's pride. I drive
through fields of icy moonlight,
remembering her tales:

the man who froze to death
trying to unlock his front door,
drunk and warm on a night like this,
until they found him in the morning—
still on his knees
with the key in his hand.
And the others, the families
who died in snowdrifts
when their cars broke down,
the farmer who dropped through
river ice with a team and wagon . . .
whole generations disappearing
into glacial nights,
and those who survive
even the stalking blizzards,
alone in unfamiliar beds,
or driving endlessly toward first light.

"Stiff as a board," she said,
"with the key still in his hand."

IV.

There is a house,
gaunt and thin as this hand I hold,
derelict for seven years—mausoleum
of mildew and shattered glass,
walls sagging together
like a child's watercolor.
Only the necessities still work:
outhouse, pump, and woodstove.
She didn't want to leave.

It was never very much,
but it was mine. A widow
nearly fifty years in that house,
but I provided.
Two sons,
and just my sewing money,
through the lean years
that never ended.
I've put aside enough
to bury me. See to it.

And the lean wisdom
garnered day to day:
don't count on much,
be neighborly, and
mind your business.
Don't take too many baths.
It weakens you.

V.

And now there is only the last visit,
there is only spring,
an alien season, and this tiled room shrinking
to a smooth point on her forehead—
the wintry shadow that will not go away,
that will not be exorcised by light.
She waits. Her hands
creep out unaware of themselves,
slowly meticulously crocheting
with imaginary threads
a tiny rosary of the years,
a blind message
where only one thing is sure:

At last and always
I am with you
in the long sleep of your waking
in the clock that rides forever in your eye
I am with you in the windy light
when the voice of our last tear is silenced
with nothing to remember
nothing to remember us by.

Father to Father

Children, Father—
how strange each day
to see more of you in me,
more of me in them.
This is one game for which
you never taught me rules,
and now as I begin to feel my age
move in me like lodestone
perhaps we have something
to talk out after all—
two old men unsure
of where it really starts or ends.

I sit up late
scratching something out
while all my darlings sleep,
and curse the noisy neighbor
or the barking dogs—
that will never wake them anyway.
This seems to be my job,
to play their night
like some resident Orpheus—
I, who still remember a father
thirty years ago at a kitchen table,
moving toward first light with
bread, hot milk, and *Reader's Digest*.
What was it that kept you up—
you, who understand
neither sons nor poems?

Perhaps this same thing I pass on,
so one day all that's given is returned.
Love? Duty? Fear? Hard words
for men who speak so sparingly.
Tonight it's time to say it, Father,
what's taken all these years:
I have daughters, you have a son.
Only the name ends here.

Libra

Your horoscope advises peace-making,
what you were born to do.
Diplomat of coffee stain and broken hinge,
you praise the falling leaves,
the coils of dust beneath your bed,
the old dog circling one last time before
she finds her place beneath your flickering lamp.
Late September moon ascending,
orange and full and wet. Mantra of worn clocks.
Empty school rooms slumber in the dark,
swollen eyes at the window.
What is it you have learned?
That you have traveled far enough
to start the journey back.
That your promises rise and fall
with weather, seasons, tides.
That the slender hammock of your sleep
is strung between two doors:
 what you'll fail to do tomorrow,
 what you've failed to do today.

Mac

"Good Egg"—her favorite words
for those she liked—beyond that,
all was Irish flare and curse.
She had a temper made for feuds
and kept her whiskey in the fridge
so she wouldn't have to fool with ice.
And when they cut her open just to find
they couldn't stop the cancer,
she went back to the nursing home
from which she'd just retired
as head night nurse—
helpless, hairless, strangely mute.
And if they ever stopped to watch
the terrible irony at work
they never seemed to show it—
condescending, starched, and vague.
Old women die of cancer every day,
even the tough and lonely ones
stripped of all but the crying out.
Was she patient here or nurse?

She used to tell stories of the ones
whose age had finally snapped—
night walkers, streakers, babblers,
old men running naked in the halls.
I never heard her speak
of those who only had to wait,
nor the hands that must have reached out.
But then, this page is cold
with all that I've forgotten,
my last and only Irish aunt:
Good night, Old Dear, "Good Egg."

Our Lady of the Table

Each year she stoops a little lower,
hair thinner, another bit of flesh fallen away.
Life is measured in decades now
and this is her tenth—the one truth
she knows for sure, from the first Amen
to the last dish scoured and put away.
"I won fifty dollars once," she interrupts,
then fades. The meal goes on,
the conversation swirls like leaves—
one end of the table, then another.
She sits at the still center
looking bewildered, regards the
tiny pile of food upon her plate
as if she knows how little good it does.
"My son quit smoking once," she offers,
and again the leaves swirl among us.
For this is Family and she
is rock, or post, or cloud,
whatever it is that none of us
has touched for years,
and this is the ritual called
Going Home, with smiles and nods.
Another meal disappears.
She stacks the empty plates
in front of her with cautious pride.
"I'm 95." Amen.
She sits among us like a prayer
that no one dares to speak aloud.

The Trouble with Cemeteries

No, I don't like them either—
from the intricate clutter of the East
to the Midwest's precise geometry—
but they always stop us, don't they?
Like this one near Elizabeth, Minnesota,
right next to the softball field.
"Hold your breath," the children say—
It's what you do when you drive past
boneyards, a little bit of death
to make the passage safe.

We drive on silently, beyond
the empty ball field near the graves.
October leaves, cold wind from the southwest.
The ancients knew it best: *obolos*,
two coins on the dead eyes
and one in the mouth. *Passage money.*
Good enough for graves and poems.
We hold our breaths.

Hopeless Case

I still can hear the name in sleep,
snagged again on the paperclip fence of
her resolve. "Daydreamer," she cried, as
I wandered in forests of black script alphabets.

Q was the one I never could get right,
a backward letter, like I could be, she said.
I wanted to scream into her thumbtack eyes
but crept away, with pigeons on the sill.

She tried to rescue me, I must say that,
through all those days of groaning clocks,
till my notebook rose and flapped away
through a tiny inkblot in the clouds.

Sometimes in nightmares we meet again,
in deserted schoolrooms full of chalky
smirks, as once again I struggle to recite
all those lessons that were never learned.

My Grandfather's Lawnmower

I can still hear the whirring, clanking—
the old lawnmower on summer mornings,
my grandfather in his vast yard,
looking up toward my bedroom window,
sliding back his hat and wiping his face.

The smell of fresh mown grass rises,
but now the lawnmower is hosed down,
hung up on its hooks in the garage.

And I, who am still hiding in my bed,
will never earn the pile of shiny quarters
on the kitchen table—
downstairs, where grandfather is
silently pulling the shades,
closing year after year of curtains
against the heat of the long afternoon.

Roadside Attraction

You can tell right off what's happening
from the fresh pine boards across the windows.
Even the old gas pump is gone,
sold last week to a man who owns a restaurant—
thinks he'll make a big fishbowl of it.
It'll be cute, he says, a real attention getter
when you walk in the front door.

Wouldn't you know, somebody stopped for gas
the very next day, lost from the interstate.
We sold him some chewing gum
and then he looked kind of sad.
Real interesting place you've got here,
he said, I'll have to stop again
sometime I'm passing through.

Nothing much left inside now—
just some shoelaces and lamp wicks,
the canned goods that never sold.
Maybe we should turn the place into a bar—
drive to Fargo and get back that gas pump.
A real attention getter is what the man said.
We could use one of those.

The Wife

"I don't know why I live with her,"
he says, trying to make the joke again.
Perhaps it's just the beer,
the lateness of the hour.

"The Wife," he says, "I really should
take her out more often"—
this quiet creature kept at home,
who used to like to dance, he says,
who squanders all her free time on the phone.

Last call. What would The Wife say
if she saw him now, leering at the
waitress checking half-filled glasses
like some willowy meter maid?

Too soon, too late, it's time to go—
back to tidy houses
where The Wife is waiting,
where children safely sleep
and one late show grows into another.

The Wife, he says, expects us home.

The Former Student

Even from the corner booth
you notice something familiar
in the bartender's eyes.
"Don't you remember me?"
The former student speaks,
reminds you how he still hates to read
the kind of books you teach.

At the lake he's the one with muscles
and the dripping tan,
the irritated waitress on the midnight shift,
the mechanic who bludgeons you
with words like compression ratio and solenoid.

A nudge, a pointing finger, and a stare,
as if you can't survive the space
outside your office walls—
he does your taxes, fixes every leak,
loads your groceries, guides you to your seat.

When you visit the clinic for the final check
on your vasectomy
he's the one in charge of sperm samples,
the teller who sniffs your paycheck,
the headwaiter leering at the holes in your socks.

Alone at last in the parking lot
you belch and sigh and scratch.
Guess who steps out from behind a parked car?

Office Hours

He comes to your office at dusk
to turn in his final paper—
the one he's resented
since before he was born.

But mostly he comes
to give you one last look—
the way he would visit a museum
if he went to museums—
to let you know somehow
that it's not very much,
this love you have for words.
He will make more money,
be freer and better and less bald.

He has it planned already.
Someday he will come back
to tell you all this—
that he hasn't changed,
that he was right all along.

Wild West

Trouble is, it's getting harder
and harder to find a good horse—
even the stage to Tombstone is a
Chevrolet. Posses and Indians
will only work for union scale,
the cavalry is fighting hostiles
on the far side of the moon.

Good whiskey must be part of
someone else's dream—most folks
in this town roll funny cigarettes.
You ever hear of dancehall girls
in pantsuits? A schoolmarm
teaching sex education classes?
Wagon trains don't stop here anymore.
No square dances in years.

On the other hand, the mayor's still
the sneaky little dude who owns most of
the ranches and the only good hotel.
You don't have to travel far to find
a poisoned well. Snake-oil shows and
lynchings happen almost every day.
There's always a gunslinger or two
ready to prove who packs the biggest gun—
out here along the windy interstates,
where our shadows stretch for miles.

Brother Blues

These are the messages for today—
bills to pay and promises,
a phone call just to say
you're dying—
whatever it is we're too old
to call temporary anymore.
Listen to the ways
our bodies fail us,
surely as wallpaper peels
or faucets drip.

You've gone out and bought
a sensible warm hat
and look just like the paper boy
you once were.
But each door on your route
hides another bad account—
the ones who never pay,
the ones who say it's not so rough,
it could be worse . . .

So what shall we call it today?
An old jazz tune
from some dim honkytonk?
Let's call it that
and walk out into winter
looking for a good all-night cafe,
and eat too much again, and wish
we could still smoke cigarettes.

The crowd of wanderers is fine tonight—
the old white beard in filthy gabardine
who dusts his seat
until the napkin frays,
the gray man in the crazy wig
who's tired, man, tired.
The streets move by us
offering light:
a little wine, imported beer,
a little Jesus
for your soul, soul, soul . . .
Whatever you need
they almost have it here.

Until it's time to say goodbye
and go back home
and wonder how it got so late,
and think about what pills to take,
perhaps a letter home to say
the weather's getting worse,
And then it starts again—
the message for today
is a broken muffler
cruising every street.

Turn up the radio a bit—
an old piano tune
you've heard someplace before.
You close your eyes and hum along.
And the faucet drips.
And the snow comes down
just as you hoped it would.

Good Friday. Just West of Here

"What a death were it then to see God die?" —*John Donne*

We drive the last dim blocks
to Ralph's, the corner bar
where old campaigners from the beet plant
pace the aisles with teenagers
and jukebox music loud as grief.
Across the river in Dakota
the bars are closed today,
so everybody's here—
even the Mary Kay lady
with her gold handbag,
who will retire when she finds
enough faces to patch up.
It's good to have a mission in life,
you know, in sunless April
when ice floes jam the river—
the young man in the buckskin fringe
says he's going to walk across
as soon as he comes down.
30 degrees with wind. Last call.
And then it's time to ride around again
and wait for signs.

The Last Time

for James L. White

I can't stop thinking of the last time I saw you—
how you looked so tired and so severe,
how I just wanted to hug you
and say it's all right, to lie a little
just to make us laugh again.
And I'd tell you if I could
that the last time should be different—
heat lightning on a warm night
and us just sitting on a front porch swing
to watch the families coming home
from the drive-in movie.
And we'd talk for hours in soft voices
'til the rain started coming down near dawn.
Then you'd go in to shut the windows
and fix us a snack
and I'd light the last cigarette,
the one we'd been saving.
And we'd think of everything we shouldn't do
all over again, and maybe then
I could get to that place
where the weeping finally starts.
No, I don't know what it means to die.
It must be quite beautiful, you say.

The Muse

It's a place I've been in before—
three calendars, all wrong,
two fans to lap the waves of smoke
from one wall to the next,
an old formica counter top
with red and black amoebic swirls
and crusted egg to bump the plates against.

Menu? she says. Her name is Melody.
You look like hot beef and fries to me.
Ashes from her Lucky Strike
tumble toward my coffee cup.

You know, I've heard all the lines
at least twice, she tells the fry cook
spread out like a stain in the corner booth.
Business has been slow.

So what'll it be? she turns and asks.
Hot beef and fries sounds fine.
Trust me, she says, and
slops the coffee to the rim and past.
I hardly ever lie.

The Trouble with Poems

Say that you are reading this poem
and something you don't want to happen
does. You remember your father
chasing you down the street with his belt.
What was it you did?
Can you remember, or were there
too many times to remember?
That's the trouble with poems.
You never really know just
where they're going to take you—
like this late afternoon light
and outside the window
fir trees laden with cones
bowing like dancers in the wind.
That's better, isn't it?
Then what about that wind,
the storm coming, the trees
disappearing into waves of snow
and you stuck somewhere miles from home
in a snowdrift, with no more than
a few minutes of gas left in the tank
that you should have filled yesterday,
but you forgot, and now you might die
alone way out here because you're stupid,
because you don't know how you'll
ever explain this to your father,
who is out searching for you.
Poems are like that, you say,
and he just looks at you and shakes
his head. If I had my belt with me,
he says, I'd teach you about poems.
And you know that he already has.

For Friends Who Send Poems

In with the blare of catalogues,
circulars in anonymous envelopes,
lurid promises of fortunes to be won,
there's a small package with my name on it,
light seeping from tears in the wrapping.
For a moment, everything stops:
I turn a book of poems over in my hands,
fingering the sheen of the cover and I see
a face beside a window, expectant,
looking up with the thinnest smile,
and at that moment I remember
just how unfaithful I am:
I will abandon each page that
calls me to one of my own—
it may take years before I finish reading.
Then I see another face by a window,
my face, and I know again that
what we give, we get back,
what we lose, someone will find for us,
and what is sent out will stay
beyond all finishing and forgetting.

North of North

Today with no surprise
the wind chill sinks to 50 below.
The mailman slouches up the walk,
head down, the way we all learn how
to walk on this far edge.
Friends write to say how cold it must be here,
and thank whatever gods they have
this weather's north of them, far north.

But we say it too—
It's always colder somewhere else.
We praise our plows and furnaces,
fall back again on what we know:
there are no last words,
and what we speak of
is neither storm nor chill,
but what would happen if all letters stopped—
that other winter, directionless,
colder than ice, deeper than snow.

FROM
MINNESOTA GOTHIC
AND
AFFINITIES

Homesteaders
for Brom Griffin

When they came
some of them already knew
that here was more than flatness;
here at last was a place
where all things would be possible.

* *

Call it ocean, call it desert;
trails move off in all directions—
tall grass, wheatfield, open range.
Everyone here is traveler.
No one knows the way.

* *

The buffalo wallow is thick with prairie aster,
coneflower, gentian, blazing star.
We walk the fields till dusk,
when deer come down to drink at the river
and a cool wind ruffles the bluestem.
The sky is full of old bones.

The Other Side

Hoods were the ones who knew
about wheels, who smoked and shaved
and even got the stuck-up girls
to turn their heads.
Like Kenny Liston in his black
leather jacket and motorcycle boots
with those half-moon cleats, years
older than the rest of us ninth-graders,
who said he kept a switchblade
somewhere up his sleeve. Kenny Liston
under the awning of the little store
across the street, chain-smoking Camels
while we watched amazed from the
windows of our history classroom.
Kenny Liston, begging my English
homework and getting it, because
it never hurt to have a friend like him
who kept the others off you in the pool.
Kenny Liston in typing class
the day the teacher said he was
hopeless, always jamming the keys.
We watched his throat and ears
turn red, and then he did it—
took the brand-new Smith Corona
to the third floor window and
pitched it out.   Later, we heard
Kenny robbed the little store and shot
it out with cops over on Clinton Avenue.
The rumors grew. He'd stolen a
beer truck and passed out samples
at Central High just up the street.
He'd taken the principal's car and

driven all the way to Florida. Who
knows the truth in ninth grade anyway?
All we cared about was that he
terrified us, that he knew what
we didn't and dared to do it.
How we hoped we could forget Kenny,
never imagining we'd be meeting him
over and over again, out there
cruising in his stolen wheels with a
back seat full of smashed typewriters,
giving the finger to all the hopeless cases
trapped behind the window glass.

Keeping the Record Straight

Each time we drove home for a visit
the first thing that my father asked about
was miles and mileage for the trip, how
long it took, the weather, road conditions—·
by the way, how are you all, those
children just keep growing up, he'd smile
at last. I learned to keep a log, cut each
rest stop a little shorter just to do better.

Of all those trips there's only one I can't forget—
tornado warnings, hail and small hallucinations
while the family slept, the wheels beneath the
casket, the slow procession west, the hill
where he was buried, near a highway.

I still keep records, though I don't know why—
something, I suppose, you do to keep awake
on those long drives back, something you do
for a father—even when you search for him
to tell the news of traveling, and he's not home.

The Love Song of J. Alfred Professor

for Roland Dille, President of Moorhead State University

The end of another term—
familiar walls of paper
line his desk again.
He's measured out his life with
what? Not coffee spoons,
not since the doctor said to quit.
Perhaps it's sentence fragments,
memos from the dean, committee
meetings where he didn't quite
speak up, his filing cabinet
full of student questionnaires.
They all say the same thing:
Keep trying. You're not there yet.

So here it is again—the clawing end
that comes with finals week.
He sits to read those papers,
knowing what he'll find:
a vast, familiar beach with lapping waves
to drive him toward a dreamless sleep—
yet here and there a drowning human voice
that wakes, surprised, and sings.
And sings!

A Man of Learning

It's always there, isn't it. Even when
I don't read the newspapers or
watch TV, it's the cancer story
I overhear at the drugstore, sad
songs on radios, faces in passing cars,
the toothless man who stops me
on my way home—to borrow the 44 cents
he's short for a bottle. You know,
he says, you looked to me like a man
of learning. He can spot us, he says,
always good for some spare change.
He's the one I wonder about tonight,
waiting for the calm between
freight train shrieks and morning birds.

You need a hobby, my father used to say,
when I'd tell him what was bothering me—
like the times they herded us to the
school basement for A-Bomb drills,
how they told us to tuck our heads
between our knees, cover necks with
hands. And how I didn't ever want to
leave those shadowed hallways, afraid
what I'd find when we got above ground.
Or maybe I didn't tell him after all.
I'll have to wonder about that, too,
fumbling for small change in the bedclothes—
and beside me, the clock radio patiently
shuffles its numbers, gathering news.

Minnesota Gothic
for David Pichaske

There's a hole in the west-bound lane,
a barricade, a sign: "Take Turns,"
it says. Take turns or you'll
never get to the Ortonville Café
and that slice of "raison pie."

Bumper stickers read "Norvegian Power"
and farmers waggle fingers as they pass
in faded pickup trucks. In the Oasis Bar
an old man in a seed hat wonders what
crops and girls are like where I'm from,
and then we settle back beneath the "Please
Do Not Throw Coins at Dancers" sign.

"Take Turns," I say. The old man grins
like a Viking. "It's quite the deal,"
he says—as the night comes
down around us filled with
dusty roads and shining eyes.

Opener

for David Pink

They're already scattered—early spawn this year,
shifting cold fronts, last night's lightning,
a threat of storms all day.
We watch the other boats patrolling,
shallow, deep, all points between—
like a task force they work,
rechecking readouts, faces, maps,
and then, far down the shoreline where nobody is,
something flashes silver near deep reeds.

Cut the motor, drift,
fling out the lines and settle back—
something's out there, who knows where?
We fish between the tricky winds
and roiling clouds, rubbing our eyes,
rubbing our backs against
the long dark months of winter sleep.

Eye of the Beholder
for Sarah

> *I've often wondered what it would be like to be*
> *beautiful. I've never had the problem.*
> —Paul Zimmer

We're always reminded, aren't we—
on every screen, on every page
we turn. Perhaps somehow we too
might find a way to measure up,
the secret of each serene gaze . . .

Today we go shopping, my fine
tall daughter and I—who looms
above the others in the store
that pause in aisles to gape
at what they think they see.

She smiles and looks at me
as if to say it doesn't matter,
even if we both know
there are times and ways it does.
But what we also know is this:

Beautiful is understanding what you
cannot ask from those who stare—
more than their eyes, more than ours.
And beautiful is finally judged
by all the reasons that you're missed.

The Penitent

What drives me from bed at first light is
a farm I visited once, and a huge black Labrador
who wore three severed duck heads
tied around his neck with baling wire—
for punishment, the farmer said, for killing
the mallards his family raised to sell.

It was a late March day, as I recall, and
.everybody went about their muddy business
except for me and that dog, watching
each other as he circled, head down
among those trusting ducks and geese,
penance flopping against his throat.

Why today should I remember that? Perhaps
it's the angle of spring sun and thawing ground
I look out upon. Perhaps it's something else,
circling with lowered eyes, bearing some stubborn,
incomprehensible grief—as that farmer kept repeating,
the only way that some of us will ever learn a thing.

Getting Used to the Water

Here's where we'll teach you
how to swim, my father said—
meaning the open lakeshore, not
the crowded bathing beaches;
meaning the drop-off
he didn't know about,
where I still watch my feet
disappearing beneath me,
still feel his fingers
dragging me up by the hair,
still choke on water in my throat.
Don't worry, my father said.
You'll learn to get used to it.

Today I fish another drop-off.
On one side of the boat
everything's clear in the shallows;
on the other, only blackness,
the unimaginable bottom.
Near shore, a family of mallards
paddles by—mother and father
with six tiny ducklings
tightly bunched between them—
to cast a larger shadow for
whatever is rising from beneath.

The Last Time
for Tom McGrath

Your room, the nurse tells me,
is the one with the scanner in it—
that, and not to be afraid to wake you.
Most patients here sleep too much anyway.

You seem to know me at first,
when you ask for a beer and cigarette,
but then all light fades and you
shudder beneath blankets, clutching
at the tubes that grow from your arm.

What are you doing here? you say.
We'll miss the dance tonight.
And how about those fences that
need mending? Have to keep them out,
you know—all of them trying to get in.

What can I do? I keep asking,
beside the small red numbers forming
on the screen above your bed.
Old friend, we've finally reached the place
each road leads somewhere else.

I'll be gone for awhile, you say—
but you keep on watching as I
bend toward you, closer and closer,
farther and farther away.

FROM
LONG DISTANCE
AND
THE WORK IS ALL

Great Plains

> *I delight in the things I discover*
> *right within reach.*
> —Ted Kooser

Try to think of one more imagination game
to keep you going, maybe what a long, dull
road trip might be compared to—like a job
you hate but need to keep to stay alive.
Or remember the dream you wake from in panic,
the one that won't let go of you for days,
its own tedious roads that keep you looping
back upon yourself. You sing along
with some melody beneath the static.

Try to remember loneliness is supposedly
the beholder's making, even as the sun
slips into heavy clouds it will not
rise from, the dark fields growing into night,
until you notice lights in the distance—
soon startled by bright beams coming at you,
the giant combines churning, the grain trucks
lining up in sheets of billowing dust.

Try to get it down, all of it—the world
within a world you couldn't imagine
'til right now—so that when you wake,
finally, you can still feel that dust
beneath your eyelids, the prairie earth
you'll need to pare from fingernails, the
disappearing road still rising up to meet you.

Prairie Storm

for John Reinhard

Driving back late from Winnipeg
we watch the border sky turn nightmare red.
All around us patches of fire and smoke
with scattered figures moving on the prairie.
A simple explanation, the customs agent says:
when the crops are in, the fields are burned.

To keep awake we listen to songs on the radio—
lost love and heartache, with bulletins of
world-wide storms, a threat of war continuing.
Easy enough to understand, isn't it?
After a harvest, what's left must burn.
All the long drive home we watch the sky for fire.

Flat Country
after Dana Gioia

Give me a landscape where the sky is huge
with scudding, booming clouds—no walls of trees
obscuring hovering hawks, except along
the riverbanks where cottonwood and willow
watch meandering currents, ox-bowed in
their own stubborn time.
                              This is a place where
fences seem an afterthought, no mountains
to distract the eye from bluestem haze and
spikes of blazing star—spirit's reckoning
that rises with each plume of dust or smoke.

Perspective is the ground that creeps up from
the valley floor, reminding us of what
is coming from a long way off—rippling
the prairie grass, another universe
that spreads out all around us, at our feet.

The Room You Go Back To

*It is all around you and inside you, and for reasons you
cannot know, it contains everything you did or felt
or thought.*
—B.H. Fairchild, from "The Memory Palace"

It was the kitchen, or a succession
of them—the places tend to disappear,
but a yellow Formica table always remains,
my father sitting there in his undershirt,
reading the evening paper, sipping
beer from a glass, and my mother
standing at the sink, washing something—
dishes or vegetables or jars for canning—
hair pressed damp against her neck
and forehead, while my little sister
squirms in her highchair or playpen,
thwacking a wooden spoon. And here
I come in my rolled-up jeans and
cowboy hat, holding a shot glass for
my ounce of Shell's or Stag or Grain Belt—
whatever beer has been on sale—which
tickles my nose and leaves an aftertaste,
while the years outside the windows
flicker by like those Burma Shave signs
on the roads my father has to travel
three weeks out of four. But for now
he turns on the red plastic radio to
what he calls a Twi-Night Doubleheader
and says again someday he'll have to
get time off and take me to a game.
But that will be a long while yet,
another kitchen, another city, another
twilit afternoon, as something frying

on the stove makes our mouths water,
and my mother smiles at her boys,
as she calls us, silent at the table
with their beer and ballgames, waiting for
the crack of a bat, the streak of light
rising against the lengthening shadows.

Original Sin

It would go on my permanent record,
the teacher said, marked in ink that wouldn't
come off, not ever—in some huge old
dusty book, I guessed, whose pages would
always follow me. What else was in it,
from how far back? I'd wake some mornings
imagining that. The strangest thing was
how soon I could forget just what I'd done—
nothing but that teacher's frowning glare,
while just behind her on the classroom wall
George Washington looked down. He never lied,
and how I hated him for that, hated
every shining example they gave me,
to which I knew I'd never measure up—
as I stood there alone beside my desk,
wondering again what she'd be writing down.

Driver Education
for Charlie

I must have been the only boy
in junior high who didn't know
a camshaft from a universal joint.
Even my friend Charlie read the
hot-rod magazines, dreamed his
mother's '56 Bel Air would someday
be a car worth cruising Lake Street in—
with a little work, you know, some
pin stripes and those rumbly pipes.
We'd learn how to lower the rear end,
too, and find something cool
to hang from the rearview mirror.

I had to admit it would be great
to have a car like that—to have it,
not to make it. Even Charlie
thought I must be nuts—
me, with my father's old '48 Ford
sitting out in the garage unused.
There, in that dim light we'd test
those strange pedals. Clutch,
he'd say. You've got to push it
down to change the gears.
What did I care about shifting
when there were stale cigars in the
glove compartment? Just let me
light one up, I'd say—with matches
I'd stolen from my mother's box above
the stove—then you can teach me gears.

He'd watch my smiles turn green
and there we'd sit, shifting and
puffing through our Saturdays.
You'll never learn to drive that way,
my friend kept reminding me, and
for those moments he was the crazy one.
Then he'd tell me to put it out. I'm
getting tired of this, he'd say. Besides,
I've still got to show you how to steer,
how to keep your stupid eyes
on the road ahead.

Eighth Grade

Our biology teacher should have known better
if anybody should. "When I call on you," she said,
"You'll stand beside your desks when you answer."
She had to know those helpless and amazing things
that kept happening in our pants, the way we boys
would slide from our desks half-crouched
and spit out just about anything, then slip back.

English was another matter, that sweet new teacher
who thought she could control us by ringing a little bell,
which tinkled constantly beneath our raucous joy.
More than once, we made her cry—
we, who couldn't seem to help ourselves.

Years later, someone said those first months
in the classroom turned out to be her last,
and now I still can see her standing there in bright,
tight-fitting floral prints, so shy and beautiful and alone.
How could she know that with biology next hour
we simply had to give her everything she never deserved?
How could we know what we met in those two rooms
were the ones who'd define us all our lives?

Music Education

for David, Bill, and Jeremy

The first time, it was Louis Armstrong
at the Kansas City auto show, where
my father took me to see the new cars—
which I mainly ignored, perched on
some shiny bumper not twenty feet from
the bell of that magnificent horn and
something so grand, even then I knew
I'd never be the same. I was fifteen,
and not long after that it was Basie,
then Ellington, with their big bands rocking
the shopping center parking lot not far
from where we lived. Hard to believe that
right here were those names from records
I'd been listening to, and soon enough
there'd be Bird and Monk and Benny Goodman
hour after hour in my room, Miles at the
Blackhawk, Brubeck and Barnett, and even
Irving Fazola, whose *Clarinet Marmalade*
I'd nearly worn right off the vinyl.
And then one day most of the records stopped.
I could blame rock and roll, or cars and beer
and all those girls we kept searching for,
or maybe the way life faded into summers
working at the flour mill with a loading crew
of down-on-their-luck musicians waiting
to be side men for whatever band might
happen through town. But there weren't many,
and it wouldn't be long till that wide-eyed boy
was heading off to college, the road
that leads farther and farther from home.
But there'd always be the music, somewhere,
the first poetry he ever knew and loved.

The Boy in the Woods

He lived behind us half a mile through trees
and wanted to be my friend—to teach me
how to recognize each kind of bark or leaf,
out stalking rabbits with bow and arrow.
Then he showed me his pellet gun,
the one time he took me back to his house,
run-down and gray among leafless branches.
The only color I remember was from
a pile of wings. I had to look them up
in my father's bird book at home—
oriole and tanager, bluejay, cardinal,
goldfinch, mourning dove—and then
I packed away my bow and arrows for good.

After that, I saw him only once, at a game,
sitting by himself in a corner of the stands,
sighting an imaginary barrel at the players.
Someone said he quit school when he turned
sixteen—for years, each time I read the papers
I'd expect to see his name and once I even
hiked back to find that house again. It was
gone, and with it most of the woods, devoured
by subdivisions spreading from the highway.
But there will always be that last time,
the pile of wings he needed to show me—
his helpless smile and then his shrugging
shoulders as he turned and walked away.

Any Day Now

Like so many of their generation,
my parents learned to live by what they had
to give up. Long after they could afford it,
they still couldn't bring themselves to buy
something not on sale. My father tore his
paper napkins in two and saved half for
another meal. My mother was an expert
on every off-brand on the grocery shelves.
And all those retirement trips they never took,
right up until the cancer robbed my father
of everything, his voice fading into
phone static, still promising that visit,
the one they were going to make any day now.

Lately, I hear that voice more and more often.
And there's the dream that sometimes comes with it,
the one where my father and I are driving
somewhere for a visit in his old black Ford,
a place I probably don't want to go,
and we never speak a word between us,
even when something amazing passes
the windows. But it's all right, because there's
still a chance we'll say something important
to each other. How I wish we understood that,
both of us back then, saving our pennies and
somehow squandering most of the rest.

On the Road

> *The only people for me are the . . . ones who are*
> *mad to live . . . mad to be saved.*
> —Jack Kerouac

Someone a lot cooler than I was
gave me a copy my senior year,
probably my friend Jerry, who owned a car
but also read a lot, even subscribed
to magazines like *Atlantic Monthly*.
However it arrived, it was the first book
to keep me up all night, and never again
would I find in print that ache so huge you
could spend your whole life running from it.

Here was a book I wanted to understand—
at the dying end of the '50s in a town
on its way to becoming a suburb,
forever poised next to that larger world
of possibility, but going nowhere.
The only sacred search for kicks I knew
was riding around all night with friends
and 3.2 beer, puffing our Pall Malls,
plotting all the far out things we were
going to do, someday, man, when
we found a way to get it all together.

What we loved best was what we didn't get,
from Zen koans to Marlon in *The Wild One*,
but even in that impossibly male world,
Brando found a girl, the greatest ache
and mystery of them all. Looking back,
perhaps it's not so strange I never got around
to wondering how my father might regard
his own life, commuting to a job he sometimes hated.

Or my mother, disappearing even then
into the shadows of her kitchen world.
They'd never heard of Kerouac, didn't go
to movies. There we were, somebody's still life,
each of us waiting for endings we knew
would never come, roads we'd never travel.

Red River Valley

From time to time, there comes a need to
drive the back roads, past meandering streams
we didn't expect, the tiny graveyards
and falling-down sheds, the lone trees
plowed around so carefully.
In a place this flat and endless,
each small variation seizes the eye.

The car tracks eastward to the gradual rise
of glacial beaches. Beyond are hills
with woods and lakes, but we turn north
along the valley's edge, a broad horizon
cradling clouds, and then to the west,
past land that holds a dozen different
kinds of hay bales. Not far from home
by country reckoning we stop beside
a field edged with a swath of zinnias—
a quarter mile of blossoms, bright-headed
in waning light. It's getting late, but
still we watch the flowers—what we
won't forget those last dark miles
where other lights come out to meet us.

Lilacs

When they came west, women brought them,
gifts, perhaps, from mothers to daughters
they knew they'd never see again—
for beauty's sake, a piece of home
to plant beside the house or ring a yard,
and make a shady place to nurture children.

Around the countryside you still
can see them growing wild in clumps
where once the farmsteads stood,
reminders of what's lost or hidden—
those necessary markers of all
that wouldn't stay cut down.

Dragging Broadway

Weekends they line up for the parade,
in from every town for miles—
six blocks up and six blocks back,
while the city debates what to do about it.
The noise, the traffic, the threat of beer
and worse, much worse, they say.
You know kids, that trick of being seen
and heard.
           The tired cop keeps watching
from his motorbike—in every passing window
another face he knows. What's there to do,
anyway? Every week the circle dance grows
longer, each car braying different songs.
The words keep changing, too, the words
keep moving like a pulse, but every
now and then an old familiar tune—
until there's nothing left again but
empty streets and small lights burning
in the safe and songless dark.

Center Café

for Tom Montag

Well, you're in town, then. The boys
from the class reunion wander in
and take their places in the corner booth,
just as they might have fifty years ago—
grayer, balder, wearing hats announcing
places far away. Their conversation
rises, falls to the inevitable—a missing
friend who worked right up until the end,
another who is long past traveling. Smiles
grow distant as their silence overtakes
the room. The busy waitress pauses,
nods. She's always known the boys.

P.O.W.

Elwood laughs alone tonight,
bellows something indecipherable.
It's funny how they always sound the
same, old men toothless in dingy bars.
Elwood squints and curses at another
empty can of Pabst. What year was it
when the Chinese swept across the Yalu
like some kind of nightmare tide?
Mother died in '56, Father '54.
Don't you remember when it was
those Air Force sons of bitches lost the war?

Elwood mutters, flaps his empty cheeks
at us, then lurches up and down the bar
in search of faces that remember howitzers.
Your fly is open, someone says but
Elwood doesn't give a damn for fly boys.
He scrubs two fingers through his ragged crewcut,
sits back down and shrugs and fumbles for
his Pall Malls in his shirt. Where were we?
Elwood says to empty beer can rows like
spent artillery shells. Where were *we*
when those sons of bitches gave away the farm?

Lines

for Joe

Out in the boat last night we watched still air
suddenly filling with mayflies—as far
as we could see or move they came in waves.
Today their delicate remains are lined
on cabin screens, and once again the air
is thick with wings, this time from dragonflies,
dark and deliberate in their searching.

A single day, the mayflies come and go,
and now we see their helpless tracks laid down
on top of water where fish keep rising.
Only by chance we notice how these lives
complete themselves—another set of lines
to read and ponder for their grace alone,
another quickly disappearing page.

Glimpses

for Thom

They'd warned us of deer on the roads—
that something was making them restless,
that we'd never see them in time. Take it
easy, they said, if you want to get home—
but there at the edge of the deepest woods,
the highway was slick with blood
and parts—hindquarters in the ditch,
the glimpse of antlers, something to
make them restless, those big semis
speeding toward cities and daylight.
We wondered aloud what the drivers
could have seen, our own car shrinking
to wheels and eyes, trying to take it easy
on that crowded road—where the only thing
to leap out startled from the dark was us.

Midway

It took a long time to buy that first ticket,
even with the dares of those few summer friends
I'd always find at the county fair. We'd ride
the Tilt-O-Whirl until we reeled and puked
whatever forbidden food we'd been eating,
but the Tilt-O-Whirl was safely earth-bound,
not like the rickety Ferris wheel, where I'd watch
amazed—that noisy belt, those greasy gears,
and high above, the small seats teetering.
It had to be ridden, I didn't know why—
with an older boy who said it would be fine,
who laughed all the way up as I clung to the bar
giddy with fear I'd never felt—until our seat crested
the top, and I knew I'd be back, again and again,
directionless above the blur of lights that stretched
to summer's end, with all those huge gears turning.

The Wall between Us

He moves in darkness as it seems to me.
—Robert Frost

Late in the afternoon of Halloween
my new neighbor stops by to introduce
himself at the front door. At first I think
it must be an early trick-or-treater—
a young father with his small son in tow,
both staring at our grinning jack-o'-lantern
and then the bowl of brightly-wrapped candy.
Take some, I say, but the father says no,
sharply—they have their own candy at home,
and besides, they don't participate in
godless rituals. He's simply here to
give me notice he's putting up a fence
between our two backyards—mostly for dogs,
he says, two Labradors who'll need the space.
But not to worry about any noise—
they'll be fitted with special collars
which will shock them if they dare to bark.
When I joke about the line *good fences
make good neighbors*, he simply stares, then says
the Lord has blessed him with a growing family.

True to his word, a six-foot-high board fence
goes up in days, followed by the dogs,
so strangely silent in their circling
and endlessly alone—I can't help feeling
glad weeks later when I hear that one of them
escaped, and gladder still to find out that
my neighbor bought the house to fix it up
for quick resale. He'll be gone by spring—
but for his pamphlets on finding the Lord,
a fence that casts long shadows in the yards,
and a small boy's eyes, darting hopelessly
from a bowl of candy to his father's frown.

Lost and Found

> *Some keep the sabbath going to*
> *church;*
> *I keep it staying at home.*
> —Emily Dickinson

Sunday morning, blues on the radio—
I know that tune too well,
buried in my chair with football scores
while all the family sleeps.
What's lost is found and lost again,
the Sunday morning paradox—
between the then and now,
the stop and start again,
a church bell and a mouth harp toll.

I sit with news I didn't want to read—
threats of war and promises no one will keep.
Furnace surges, snowflakes gather
on the window sill, a jet plane rattles glass,
and all the house is fast asleep.

Winter Count
for Jay and Martha

Each summer I keep the bird book close,
though pictures rarely look like what I see—
colors not quite right and variations
much too similar to choose from. These past
few winters I've hung a feeder near the
kitchen window and watched pine siskins
every day, the birds I knew would come.

This year the snow's too deep for me to reach it—
the feeder hangs empty, swings in wind,
the only thing I'm certain will return, while
leafless hedges fill with sparrows celebrating sun—
like train whistles, those steady choruses
I don't usually hear. It takes a visitor to tell me
what a noisy place I choose to live in,
or to notice that snow shovel in the garage,
the one half-eaten from years of scraping walks.

Sparrows, shovels, and the cries of trains—
what's always there but seldom seen,
and now, these words so tentative across
the stark notebook pages, retrieved
from where I left them weeks ago.
Before spring thaw I'll send them out—
to friends who live beside a frozen lake,
whose own bird book lies well-thumbed
on a sunny table, who also know in seasons
cold beyond belief how the most familiar
sounds and movement call us back so suddenly
from places we've forgotten having been,
to clear at last each drifted-over path.

Memory Care Unit

"I don't know where I'm supposed to be,"
she says, beginning her rosary of
wringing hands. If past is prologue,
then tomorrow is the day that never comes.

Myrtle simply babbles, fiercely
carpet sweeping clean wood floors
while Alma's off again to find
the sister she knows is waiting
somewhere just behind closed doors.
Jean's the cheerful one, proud to
remember piano tunes across the years
but not the face she talked to last.
"Where are you from?" she asks and
then replies "that's good" to every answer.

Enter here a world of women alone so long
they gather round each visitor, transfixed
by the flicker of something almost familiar,
as if whispers alone can hold them up.

"Where am I supposed to be?" she asks,
trusting me for any answer. I take her hand
and we recite those necessary names again:
mother, son, right here, right now, and *always.*

Housman's Grave

And I will friend you, if I may
In the dark and cloudy day.

The roads are narrow through the Shropshire hills,
where Sunday bells have ceased their faithful toll.
Gray skies seem fitting here, deserted towns,
and then the shrine at Ludlow, carved in stone
at St. Laurence's church. Beneath the name
and dates, someone has laid a laurel wreath
atop a garland of spring's briefest white—
for you, who pondered fame and loss so well,
who taught us heart and craft of elegy.
The valley darkens as we drive away
to meet road signs with names we somehow know,
carrying with us the words of a friend—
flowering branches on the shadowed slopes.

Oblate

Whitby Abbey, Yorkshire

Atop these bluffs above the sea, Hilda,
prioress, found this holy place, whose bare
ruined walls still rise beyond two hundred steps
some pilgrims choose to climb up from the town—
from beige to gold in morning light, beside
the lichen-covered gravestones listing back
through centuries along this windy coast,
inscriptions long ago erased by salt.
Caedmon was buried here—poet, brother,
whose name I choose to bear if not his faith.

The stark sun climbs as tour buses snake
their way along the slopes. In the car park,
as we prepare to leave, police have come
to search for teenaged boys with air rifles.
Nothing changes, after all—divine and
human always intertwined. Behind us,
where we didn't walk, Benedictine monks
are gathering for holy offices
no matter what visitors might come and go,
praying even now, for the likes of us.

The Far Shore

Waterville, County Kerry

The massing storm that seemed to follow us
along the narrow mountain roads
has finally broken, not far to the north—
black sky and lightning moving out to sea.

And now the calm of rooms above the beach,
low tide and miles of sand in flat sunlight,
though soon enough, the breakers rumbling in
as other storms sweep by us in the night.

From this far coast the cold Atlantic
stretches out toward home, ever westward,
that unimaginable place so many here
have looked to, beyond all hope of return.

Today, we've come as far as desire and roads
allow. Tomorrow, we'll turn back to plans
and traffic. For now, dreams rise with the tide
and waves breaking at the end of the earth.

Work in Progress

Paris

A lovely day for strolling down the Champs
beside a dozen quaint sidewalk cafés
where writers, mostly in berets, are busy
with their notebooks, a glass of wine, pernod—
you can't help feel you've entered more than one
novel, story, poem, perhaps to linger there—
tall man with gray beard, curious, looking like
he has no better place to go. Beyond,
near every monument, the beggars wait—
mostly girls, who hand you soiled pages
speaking of fear for their unborn babies,
the need to get back home, wherever
home might be imagined. All around you
as you walk, words on paper, theirs and yours—
so many different languages and yet
in every one a story that you know.

Finding My Way

Because I can't sleep in hotel rooms
I've come to use ear plugs and pills,
and sometimes when I wake
at four in the morning, I'm startled
by the waves of my own blood
breaking on the shores of my eardrums.

Today there's that sound again,
only I'm home, in my own bed
and it's long past sunrise. It has
to be snow, a lot of snow in the night
muffling the waves of traffic
on the busy street at the corner.

Can you blame me if I don't get up
and look? How rare it is to be
certain of exactly where you are,
to fall back asleep free of panic,
and dream, perhaps, of a lake
in August, curtains flapping
from an open window, and beyond,
the pulse of wind in leaves and water.

Two Poetry Readings

Lawrence, Kansas, 1966

1. An Evening with the Master

The name, of course, still fired my memory,
or maybe I went just because it was free,
surprised, at any rate, to find the
college auditorium half empty
for Basil Rathbone, in the fading flesh,
sharing poetic treasures from the past,
the man who'd amazed us as Sherlock Holmes
in all those classic films—on stage, alone,
with an easy chair from someone's office,
small table, lamp, and oriental rug,
a kind of dingy living room to match
his well-worn double-breasted movie tux.
An hour and a half he paced and posed—
what they used to call an elocutionist—
belting out the oldies, from Poe's raven
to Keats's urn, until that famous voice
began to fray, and all the footlights dimmed,
back across those years of dreadful horror flicks
and cameos, while he stood there, hands clasped,
smiling gauntly in shades of black and white—
one of those living legends we could tell our friends
we saw one night—and nevermore.

2. The Homecoming

A lot of students went to the reading,
perhaps because we'd heard of Langston Hughes—
a man close to tears that afternoon, for
being praised and welcomed back to Kansas.
And then he read us poems about the days
when civil rights weren't yet a movement,
holding us with the painful grace of what
we knew was right, all of us, even the
full professor who'd dozed through most of it
then asked about a theory for those short
poetic lines our speaker pioneered.
Hughes just smiled at him and shook his head,
then told us when he started publishing
his poems and found they paid him by the line,
he'd chopped every one in half to make the
poem longer. The full professor snorted
and the rest of us roared, carried away
by something unforgettable—those words,
even then, we knew we'd keep coming back to.

Occupational Hazards

I'm a poet. Catastrophe is actually
good for my work.
—Andrei Codrescu

Perhaps you've heard how we set out each morning
to scan the skies for tornado clouds, the woods for
careless sparks, the streets for ruptured mains.
We've divorced all our spouses—a few good lines
squeezed out of each—estranged our parents and
children alike. What bastards we are, they say,
and we can't deny they're right. Maybe if we wrote
stories, there'd be some way out of it, some god
from the machine chiseling escape tunnels
beneath tsunami waves or percolating lava.
The really hard part, of course, is never knowing
where it will be coming from—whatever falls from
the skies—hoping it will wipe out thousands.

Lessons

Writing is hard and writers need help.
—Richard Hugo

Strange how it all comes back from time to time,
the night you read here more than thirty years ago
and called to ask if I could drive you to
the place you'd read the next night, eighty miles
away. Who could have known that we'd be stopped
by blowing snow or that we'd have to wait
beside the interstate 'til it let up,
the only storm that never worried me
for I had an hour of stories, talk of poems—
the streets you walked in failing mining towns,
the times your life broke down, and Italy,
the field of wind you wrote about the day
that you got lost in '44, a young airman
who was taking notes he never dreamed would
one day bring him fame—and then, that other
young man listening, who never would forget
the way you said all art is failure, though
our poems mean that we somehow have a chance,
the way that sudden storms can change our lives,
remind us just what does and doesn't count.

Reply

> *For all the history of grief*
> *An empty doorway and a maple leaf.*
> —Archibald MacLeish, from "Ars Poetica"

Perhaps I never understood those lines
and maybe never will.
An *empty doorway*: what once was there
and now is lost to all but memory.
A maple leaf: I turn the image
in my head and start with green,
though it's never green for long.

Today we drove two hundred miles
to look at leaves. It's what we do
each fall, wherever we are—
what the children joke about,
this need for leaf-watching.
But not just any leaves: the maple
soars in red, from earth to fire to blood.
And then, in the day's last slant of sun
a kind of respite, more than grief,

that we too might return in a new season.
And now, as winds rasp through the trees,
I have to say good night again
to this empty doorway, this stubborn page,
another leaf—turned, unturned, and turning—
in all this dark, a spot of glowing red.

Absences

> *Even when you are not in a room, you are*
> *in it, your voice everywhere.*
> —Bill Holm, 1943–2009

The message that's recorded on the phone
is unmistakably bad news, and then
another call tells us it's one we love—
a sudden death while traveling, somehow
appropriate for one who always
seized life too completely to stand still.

A door slams shut, a wall has dropped away,
and once again I'm driven back to
empty pages, insufficient words,
to rooms he always filled on entering—
rooms of books, piano music, and good friends,
who raise their glasses one last time.

Now, as all the lights are blinking off
in every prairie town we've ever loved,
when all the toasts are made and songs are sung,
when leaving is the only certainty,
a single voice keeps echoing, along each
dark, well traveled hallway of the heart.

The Work Is All

Any day's writing may be the last.
—Roland Flint

It's taken the death of an old friend, a poet,
to drive me back to these notebook pages
I'd abandoned, to puzzle out in words
what my heart seems so dumb to.
But words are the places we've lived,
he and I—if not wisely or greatly,
then with amazement and even, sometimes,
that grace we didn't know we'd been given.

"The work is all," he said in a poem,
knowing too well how little will get read—
but also the need to send a prayer each day
for all those good words that manage to come,
especially now, as the waning winter light
dapples notebook sheets and books of poems alike,
that place where old friends smile and weep together.

FROM
IN HARM'S WAY
AND
PERMANENT RECORD

The Trouble with Daydreams

A necessary shield for everything that
threatened me, I learned quite young
the power of escape, the way that almost
anything could provide it, at least for a
little while. Take these marbles clicking
in my pocket—aggies, clearies, cat's eyes,
and the treasured steelie shooter ready for
our recess games. I know the sheen of
each and every one that's turned between
my thumb and forefinger, stopped a moment
by the pang of memory—the day I dropped
my favorite and it bounced and rolled between
the desks right up to Teacher's feet. All she said
was what would hurt the most, how she expected
more from me, much more, and then that
deep green friend had found a sunless home
somewhere inside her desk. Here, at least,
light floods the window sills, the shouts as
someone's shooter stops just inches from
that little pit we've dug, filled with our
hard-won marble antes. Winner takes all, and
as we watch another shooter roll, my turn's next—
maybe today will be my lucky one. Hoping is
what I'm good at, after all, as everyone gathers
to see the stash I've for the moment won, and
I still keep picturing the one that rolled away.

Cautionary Tale

Beyond the field of grazing, gazing cows
the great bull has a pasture to himself,
monumental, black flanks barely twitching
from the swarming flies. Only a few strands of
wire separate us—how could I forget
my childhood terror, the grownups warning
that the old bull near my uncle's farm
would love to chase me, stomp me, gore me
if I ever got too close. And so I
skirted acres just to keep my distance,
peeking through the leaves to see if he still
was watching me, waiting for some foolish move—
those fierce red eyes, the thunder in the ground—
or maybe that was simply nightmares. It's
getting hard to tell, as years themselves keep
gaining ground relentlessly, their hot breath
on my back, and not a fence in sight.

Hidden Agenda

Today, it's tuna hot dish—the kind
with crumbled potato chips on the top.
Lovingly, my mother pulls it bubbling
from the oven—golden, greasy, salty,
a small boy's surest sense of succulence.

But everything we eat lately seems to take
a can of Campbell's Cream of Mushroom soup,
and I hate mushrooms. Isn't it funny,
my mother says, when mixed with other stuff,
even things we don't like taste pretty good.

I don't want to agree, picking out the
tiniest bits of black, but knowing she's right.
It's always been like this with hot dish.
Casserole is what the old woman downstairs
calls it, stuffy-sounding, needing candles—

like lying down is better than going to bed,
and rolls taste better than buns. Tomorrow,
some sort of spaghetti hot dish, probably
using a can of mushroom soup, as well.
What else, I don't even want to guess.

Soldiers of Misfortune

We called ourselves the Bachelors' Union,
as if in sixth grade we had some other choice.
A few of the girls in our room had a club, too,
cryptically titled with initials from their names.
Of course, we all vowed lives of independence,
but even in sixth grade things were happening
we didn't begin to understand—like boys
waiting for girls after school to walk them home
or wash their faces in the snow. Oh, we were clever,
all right, making those anonymous phone calls,
intercepting notes and breaking codes.
But the one we couldn't begin to decipher
was seventh grade, looming like some giant
troop transport at the end of our pathetic
runway, soon to blare the boarding call
for our next deployment—another of those
missions where we wouldn't stand a chance.

Saturday Matinee

What I remember best is all the noise,
that long slope of faces rising behind us
from our favorite seats in the fourth row.
Fifteen minutes before the lights are dimmed
and the sacred curtains part, and we've
already eaten our Rootbeer Barrels and
Milk Duds, spilled our Cracker Jacks and Cokes,
and now, everything beneath us sticks.

Most Saturday afternoons are like this—
ten cartoons and then Roy or Gene or Lash,
Cisco and Pancho, or even Tim Holt,
who's my favorite, because he doesn't sing,
doesn't look like he comes from a dude ranch.

Each week, we wait for the surprises blared
by Previews of Coming Attractions,
when cheers are the loudest—for cowboys
and Bowery Boys and jungle boys, for
fat guys with skinny guys, and Stooges—
for here, beneath cascading popcorn boxes
and crushed ice, is our weekly glimpse into
the only promised land we've ever known.

All the way home, gunfights and swordfights,
varmints headed off at passes, and barroom
brawls with chairs broken across scrawny backs.
And even when the cheering finally fades,
when it's time again for parents and school,
there are still those flickering reminders
that all disbelief can be suspended,
that next time will be the best time of all.

In Harm's Way

for Clarence and Patricia

No, I didn't write on myself as a child,
no matter that my wife thinks all kids did.
All I remember is a grownup told me
I'd get cancer from the ink or pencil lead
and die, just as I would from pneumonia
after going out with a wet head. But it was
my classmates who gave me all those other
useful youthful cautionary tales, like
swallowed seeds sprouting in your stomach,
swallowed bubble gum sticking parts of your
insides together, or excess frowning
causing permanent damage to your face.

How in the world did we ever survive?
Even today, all these years later,
you can tell us by our cavernous looks,
our gurgling guts, the tiny tendrils
that won't stop sprouting from our ears.

Acolyte

Father forgive us for what we may do.
You forgive us and we'll forgive you . . .
—John Prine

Today, at the funeral I attended, the Lutheran minister
had me squirming in my seat again, expectations
rising and falling with each false ending. Dearly
Beloved, they used to begin the sermons, but I
knew there'd be nightmares. Where was that
loving God they talked about in Sunday school?

One year, thanks to junior high Confirmation class,
I even had to sit up front in a red robe and starched
white surplice—not chosen for my piety but for
being tall enough to light the altar candles.
Most Sundays, my only prayers were that those
flickering flames wouldn't go out and embarrass me.

Up front where people could watch me during
the service, I was desperate not to doze off.
As I counted rows of bricks, bald heads, or ladies' hats,
I'd try to block that tedious voice by imagining
Sunday dinner and the ballgames on TV.

Back in the sacristy at last, with stacks of old
programs and the leftover wine and wafers,
I'd joyfully strip off my uniform, numbering
the weeks until I wouldn't have to come back.

All Hallows Eve

for Glenn the Snowbird

There won't be weather like this again 'til spring,
we say, a dozen mowers roaring through
the neighborhood. It's autumn's last nice day,
and now, like all who've been condemned
we meekly await tomorrow's icy plunge
to winter, here at last. How we love it.
What else is there as interesting to talk about?
Even those of us who'll get away to
someplace warm will check the weather channel
every day for news of home—something we'll
be able to share, and gloat about.
Cold front's due tomorrow, bristling with wind,
the threat of sleet, or even snow, and how
we love remembering all those years when
it's been worse by now, far worse—like the one
when they had to cancel trick or treating.
How we love what we know we can count on.
Not long now and it will really start getting bad.

Amsterdam

One of those places where anything can happen,
from lurid sex shops and hookers posing in
windows to relentless graffiti and pot cafés.
On every thoroughfare I'm swept up by armies
of the young with backpacks, and down the street
from my hotel I meet one of them shooting up
beside a cavern of trash bags in an alley.
He follows me and flaps his arms, squawks,
and tries to take off like one of the herons
cruising for scraps among tethered houseboats
along the Singel Canal. As the street empties
I slow my pace, still careful to watch where
I'm going, the tall canal houses lined up
as if posing for a gallery portrait, while the
sun turns deeper orange as I find my way,
holding my breath, testing my clumsy wings.

At Blue Cloud Abbey

for Brothers Benet, Christopher, and Gene, OSB

Matins

Sunlight creeps along the windowsill,
the news another night has been survived—
our fast is broken with a burst of bells!

Day Prayer

Organ music spilling down the steps
and through the hallways—brief reminder
there are times when everything needs to stop,
as voices raise above themselves in praise.

Vespers

Here's the silence we've mostly forgotten.
With every breeze, the intricate patterns of
prairie grass remind us of another life.

Beside the path, the small lake holds the
last light of evening, seeping into shoreline—
one day, all we'll have to take with us.

Vigils

The distant valley's full of shimmering light,
and far above the deepening red haze
a single evening star against the black—
one last call to all that lies beyond us.

The Feast of St. Benedict

March 21

I head downstairs to put the coffee on
and stop at every window that I pass
to watch the early light obliquely break
across the dark panes of a neighbor's roof,
and curls of smoke, the day's first prayers.

Surprisingly, there's been snow in the night,
and now the kitchen windows open on
a backyard full of tracks, a fat rabbit
twitching by the budding lilac bush and
bobbing finches crowding at the feeder.

For this moment there's not a thing I want,
nothing to possess—not even the rose
in its slender vase glowing on the sill,
or just above the trees, returning geese—
and then the kettle singing on the stove.

Bird Count

for George Roberts

Scarcely September and the leaves begin
to turn—soon enough the V's of geese will
thrill us again, 'til we're left with bare branches
and huddling sparrows, siskins, chickadees—
familiar companions so easily ignored,
their cries as fierce and stubborn as our own.

Prayer before a Group Poetry Reading
for Tony Oldknow

Lord, let me not follow, please,
the guy who imitates an auctioneer,
the woman now unpacking her guitar,
the ones who've memorized their lines
or leave as soon as they have read,
and any who have recently reclaimed their lives.

Deliver me from frantic, rustling pages
and dedications to Kahlil Gibran,
from works in progress right up to
the moment when it's time to rise,
from pounders of pianos, mumblers, stumblers,
shouters, chanters, chatters—and every line
designed to bring down this or any other house.

Finally, of course, grant me the strength
not to be too pleased with myself,
and through it all to keep my commentary dry—
especially for all who think ten pages is
five minutes, and anyone who reads just one more poem
and then another short one, or a few, and then,
because we've all been so patient, this new one,
and another, just one more . . .

The Memory of Water

Here where the Sheyenne joins the Red—
upstream, the Bois de Sioux, and down,
the Buffalo—imagination finds its way
in swirls of white stirred by the prairie winds.

These are the places towns were built,
water flowing underneath snow-covered ice
laced with tracks of skis and snowmobiles
and creatures rarely glimpsed by passersby.

Today I'm home from a desert visit,
where a week of rain had finally broken—
arroyos carried everything away
except for pools on asphalt roads.

How inevitably it all flows off and disappears—
water and what it has been named for—
here, in this glacial lakebed where I live,
still dreaming of the great herds passing.

Holiday Greetings to L.A.

Thin sheets of ice are forming on the river,
inching out from shore, circling every
downed limb—tentative for the moment,
but all too soon thick enough to walk on,
assuming that you'd dare to, of course.
This is a land that knows how to kill you—
not that our deaths are any grimmer than yours,
just colder. How we envy your movie sets,
those perfect shredded plastic snowflakes
and breath that never steams in supposedly
freezing weather. But let's face it, even
here, where we're known for seasons,
forests of fake trees keep springing up
wherever we look, to say nothing of the
Christmas music we've been listening to since
Halloween. All forecasts, of course, are for
cold and snow, continuing. You know how we've
always counted on you—the way you think
we must be out of our minds to live here,
the way you can't believe we'll last 'til spring.

Artifacts

When my uncle came home from WWII
it was no surprise he brought some souvenirs,
including a German soldier's belt buckle
bearing the inscription "Gott Mit Uns."
When I was old enough to ask, my mother said
it meant "God's with us," shook her head
and sadly smiled. Most of my classmates
thought it was pretty neat for Show and Tell,
but some of the girls teased me about that
"got mittens" buckle I was so proud of.
Some of the boys wanted to know more about
the dead Kraut my uncle hooked it from,
though I tried to explain he was a medic
and probably didn't do stuff like that.

Years later, in my confirmation class,
Luther, Hitler, and Kaiser Bill formed a kind of
weird triumvirate in my head, so I asked
the minister what he thought of that phrase, though
what he said is lost, just like that souvenir itself.
Still, every time I watch the TV news it's there again.
God has been marching with someone's army,
winning football games, providing miracles
for reasons no one seems to understand.
"Gott Mit Uns"—the motto never seems to change,
no matter what language it's spoken in, no matter
what banners invoke those mysterious ways.

The Way it Works
   for Camie

You never know what you're going to find—
old letters, disintegrating newspaper clippings,
sheafs of Xeroxed poems, especially those that
inspired you to one of your own—the way
it works, when it works. Today it's a small box
of your mother's that's been in the basement
for years. No reason to open it now,
beyond some kind of listless curiosity.
Inside, there are more clippings, mostly
weddings and funerals, old contracts,
a note from a brother on his way to war
in '43, and even a letter she saved from you
in your seven-year-old's unwieldy pencil—
news of rain at your grandparents' house
far away, your summer small-town world
of county fairs and front porch swings
and finally being able to walk all alone
to the post office for the daily mail.
"I do not want you to send me any more
clothes," you gravely write, not saying why,
followed by XOXOXO for mother, father,
baby sister. The most important is what
you've saved for last: Grandma's made two
kinds of cookies and some donuts, too.
You can still smell them and always will—
the way it works, when it works. And for now,
you'll save that box with all the rest, again.

The Doctor's Daughter

Come and get me
Don't forget me
Come and get me
Don't forget me
Come and get
This silly old lady

Today once again she talks in rhyme,
chants in rhyme, shouts in rhyme,
washed up from some far shore—those years
she was an elementary school teacher, perhaps,
or some childhood game more real
than this room with its unwatered plants,
its dusty family of framed photographs,
its padded wheelchair and hospital bed.

There was an old woman
Who lived in a shoe
She didn't know what
She should do, do, do

Upstairs and downstairs
In her nightgown
There is an old woman
Who runs through the town

Tell the others where I am, she says,
ever-cheerful smile beginning to crumble.
Where am I supposed to be? she says.
It's getting dark again, and who
will tell her where she needs to be?

Good night
Sleep tight
Bed bugs
Won't bite
In the early
Morning light

Child of a physician, she knows about
hospital beds and patients, all those times
she helped out in his office, all those visits
she made with him, just to keep him company,
sometimes with a horse and buggy to a farm
so far out in the sticks she thought they were lost,
singing together his favorite hymn.

This is my story
This is my song
Praising my savior
All the day long

Don't you know how good it is to have a friend,
she says, to have the Lord there with you
all the day long and the long night too,
especially when there's nothing else to do?

And He walks with me
And He talks with me
And He tells me I am his own

Her father used to walk with her sometimes—
the one who always stood up for her, even
when she sneaked out to have her hair bobbed
like some kind of Flapper, her mother said.

There was a little girl
Who had a little curl
Right in the middle of her forehead
And when she was good
She was very, very good
But when she was bad she was horrid

It was her father who always indulged her,
except maybe that day at the lake when
he wouldn't let her try to land that lunker
she had hooked all by herself, which still tugs
on that line, doubling the pole, circling, diving,
just beneath the boat, until her father
takes the pole and slowly reels the monster in,
and even claims it, like it's *his* fish—
the one thing she can't seem to forgive him.

Come and get me,
Don't forget me
Treat me right
And I won't fight

Her mother, who once was a celebrity
in their small town, has receded into
the deepest shadows, off playing bridge
with her friends, off shopping, or simply
drinking coffee and gossiping, and now
there's just enough time to get dinner
in the oven, before her mother gets home.

Old Mother Hubbard
Went to the cupboard

Polly put the kettle on
We'll all have tea

Don't you know how she hates having to
do her mother's cooking and housework?
Don't you know she'd like to go somewhere, too,
maybe for a ride in her friend's new roadster,
back in the rumble seat with you-know-who,
not stuck watching her little brother
who can never keep from running off somewhere,
like the time they were visiting relatives
in some big city, and the only thing
that stopped him, that saved him, were all those
fascinating lights on a theater marquee,
a little like the county fair each summer.

> *Come and get me*
> *Don't forget me*

> *Come and take me to the fair*
> *Don't you know that I'll be happy there*

But there's no traveling now, no visiting,
no getting away. At the party for her
93rd birthday, the pile of cards keeps
appearing and then the cake and ice cream
and then the cards again and then the cake . . .

> *Little Bo Peep*
> *Lost her sheep*

> *Little Jack Horner*
> *Sits in the corner*

And now there are the ones who drool and smear
their food, the ones who coo, the ones who
always want to move her, and sometimes, too,
the one who rubs her back and holds her hand,
who might be husband or son or brother—
one of her favorite relatives.

Call, don't fall
Is what the sign says
Call, don't fall
Call, don't fall

Is it any wonder her voice is hoarse,
raspy, as she repeats her messages
   Come and get me
again and again, as loud as she can
   Don't forget me
eyes closed tight and chin thrust out
   Come and get me
head bobbing to the rhythm of the words
   Don't forget me

Who will tell her where she needs to be?
Who is going to come and take her hand?

In loving memory of Bernadine Call Vinz, 1912–2006

Assisted Living

The second-graders came again today
to sing and smile and let the shaking hands
caress them, let vacant eyes keep scanning
for some sign—who might these children be and
where will they go now, and did you know that
sometimes it's the lady with her dogs
who visits? They liked to be stroked too.

Tomorrow, the Message Board announces,
there will be songs and crafts and God is Love.
Now, they're showing videos of Lawrence Welk,
and then at last it's time to eat again.
Stop by some other day you want to feel
you're being useful. Bring something to eat,
something to coo over, something to pet.

The Way We Said Goodbye

So many years later, the old dog
still circles, head lowered, crippled by
arthritis, nearly blind, incontinent.
We repeat the litany, as if we need
convincing that the end is right.

I'll get her an ice cream cone if you'll
drive her to the vet, my wife says.
So there we sit on the front steps
with our friend, and in the car, as always,
when she senses the doctor's office
drawing near, she moans and tries to
burrow underneath the seats.

What remains, the memory of how
she taught us all the way we need
to learn to live with wasting.
There we sit, together, one last time
as all that sweetness slowly disappears.

Professor Emeritus

So, how's retirement treating you? they ask,
and there's still no good answer—I keep on
learning, day to day, just what it is I miss,
or thought I would and don't, or don't and should.
Maybe I'll start mentioning those teacher dreams
that come more often now—all those rooms I
still can't find, the missing lecture notes,
the blank-faced class I fail to recognize.

Tomorrow will be Christmas Eve. I'm up
before first light, the rhythm of the seasons
still what drives me from my bed—all papers
finished, grades turned in, and now a little
time to savor momentary silences.
Yesterday, a former student met me
with a hug, another slapped my back in
the supermarket line, full of season's cheer
and maybe something more. I have to wonder
what they still remember after all these years,
but glad they still remember it at all.

A Glass, Darkly

for my father, Leland Vinz, 1909–1985

Each morning as I ease arthritic
aches from bed, I can hear my father
in the dim hallway ahead of me,
that string of childhood markers
I've come to call his sound—groan
and sigh and throat cleared in the
bathroom mirror, where once again
we hail each other, still tentative,
eyes shifting to any convenient corner.
Maybe now I've finally come of age,
hand raised toward the glass, fingers
slowly reaching toward themselves.

A Certain Age
for Bill Tilland

Perhaps it's no surprise I've been dreaming lately of
those black and white cowboy films I used to love,
the ones with fantastic chases on horseback
which usually ended with a shootout in the rocks—

the ones we knew the good guys would survive
no matter what the odds might be, where,
give or take a flesh wound in the left arm
or a slightly grazed skull, villains always missed.

Even then we couldn't help wonder why our heroes
never had to reload but cheered ourselves hoarse
anyway, for each and every scripted impossibility—
all those things we knew couldn't last.

Today the subject is biopsies and scans,
different images on Technicolor screens,
and those familiar pings and whines of ricochets
suddenly louder, almost close enough to feel.

NEW AND
UNCOLLECTED
POEMS

Still Life with Tulips

The woman at the supermarket floral counter
asks me if I know that tulips are the only flowers
to keep on growing after they've been cut.
Maybe it was just to get me to buy some and
see for myself, which I did—their heavy heads
now drooping toward the kitchen counter from
their pottery vase of water, half an inch longer
than yesterday—a bunch of bright yellow flowers
on an otherwise dreary day, even more beautiful
the way they keep holding on for dear life.

The Art Historian

for Katie at the Musée de l'Orangerie, Paris

Room after room, the Monet water lily murals
surround us on the walls. The crowd today
is restless, filing past distractedly, then
stopping for a random moment here and there.
Even the well known actor goes unrecognized,
like all of us wandering our own paths.
Bored children gallop in and out among the legs
and frowns just as they've always done, lovers
strike a longing pose as if on cue, a few note-takers
work up close, while others find places to sit.
And then we come upon our daughter weeping,
on a bench, alone, overcome by what she sees
and what she knows, in ways the rest of us
will never know or see, lost among the
waves of light from Monet's water lilies.

Working Out

Tonight is truly winter, clear and sharp,
and as I pass the glassed-in fitness center
on my way home, I notice a solitary figure,
hard at work on one of the elliptical machines—

an older man, perhaps my age but probably younger,
which is usually the case. He works his legs furiously,
as if he might catch whatever most eludes him,
by determination alone. I wave and almost

stop the car and go inside to tell him I've seen something
here tonight I'm going to write about, an image
that will stay in my head like the café in Hopper's painting
Nighthawks, which maybe he doesn't even know about.

For a moment I can picture his bewildered face
as he glances around, to see if we really are alone. But then,
beyond the rising price of gas and the recent cold snap,
what else would there be to talk about, much less share?

I'd no doubt have to make apologies, retreat
through the maze of my own hapless words,
leaving him to his solitary machine once more, and
me to mine, driving past the soon-deserted parking lot.

Good Sport

When you were fat and tall
and couldn't jump, you played
center in basketball—your job,
the coach said, to clog up the lane,
take charges, practice free throws.

When you were slow and batted left
you played right field, hit next to
last but got on base a lot by getting
walked or beaned, or swinging late.
They expect you to pull, the coach said.

What he didn't say was even if
your dad had been a star athlete
and taught you well, even if
you subscribed to *Sport*, knew stats,
and watched the TV games religiously,

you'd never look back fondly
at hero-rides shoulder-high.
Still, it was worthwhile, wasn't it?
Knocked down again, flat on your back,
looking up into the coach's eyes

and shrugging everything off, then
grinning, just as you'd been taught.

Sins of the Fathers
for GK the DJ

My daughter wants the car tonight, no,
needs the car tonight—to go somewhere,
to do some things, you know, be back
before it gets too late of course,
if I say so, which I usually do,
of course. I trust her—it's the others
I don't trust, the others I worry about,
and round we go again.

Headlights pass the driveway—
I study every shadow on the wall,
each voice from the dark street,
and laughter—faint, familiar
laughter, rising and falling
on every breath of wind.

Elegy for Clifford

He was the only honorary Irishman at
the Chatterbox Bar, usually speaking
Gaelic, or so we thought. We later found
he was simply drunk and muttering behind
those everlasting smiles, though maybe he'd
recite Yeats, mostly in English, or even
Eliot. By closing time, who could tell?

The night the place finally shut down
the regulars gathered to say goodbye,
along with the local beat cop and a few
NP Avenue wanderers drawn like roaches.
When Clifford suggested we should sing,
the only song we all knew the words to
was "God Bless America," which we sang as
loudly as we could—and then, the last call,
the golden light growing dim, the farewell
waves from our ageless waitress in the white,
knee-high boots she wore in any weather.

Clifford simply disappeared, for then and
evermore, quoting his own Gaelic version of
whatever poem he could imagine.
I still think of him whenever I drive past
the place that old bar used to be—gone,
like so much else, but as they say, as long as
your words are remembered, you're still alive.
Dear Clifford, I can't help hoping that it's true.

Late Summer Song

Heat lightning stalks
the long tunnels of interstate.
For a moment I put on the
discarded clothes of childhood,
and everything is large and far away—
a hand to hold my cheek against,
a lamp that burns all night.

Home is where I go toward fall,
and each year something else is stripped away—
a time when everything speaks of endings,
of being one more time a kind of total guest,
worn and quiet and utterly at peace.

Bookcase

Childhood is the first shelf,
splashed with the colors of
comics and book-ended by tales
from two stiff-backed grandmothers.
One of them told me soft drinks
would rot my insides, just like the big
nail she'd dissolved in a bottle of Coke.
The other didn't hold much hope
I'd live at all. If I didn't choke to death
on a fish bone, the pneumonia from
sleeping in drafts would do the job.

Farther down is *Mad* magazine, and then
the *Playboys* a friend stole from his father,
and the Hardy Boys, whose lives I longed
to live, until the worlds of science-fiction,
pretty much filled up the next two shelves.
It gets too complicated to go much farther.
All I didn't learn in school might be there,
the pile of classics I meant to read, and
a couple of college texts I couldn't begin
to fathom. Maybe even a few more of my
grandmothers' cautionary tales. Beyond
that, who knows? Maybe empty shelves.

Metaphysics

for Orv

My friend told me not to worry about
bringing bait. For some strange reason
there were plenty of small frogs
on the beach by the cabin, perfect for bass.
And there were, hundreds of them, so
we scooped a couple of dozen into a bucket,
feeling good about our luck. My friend showed me
how to hook them through the mouth, their hands,
or whatever they're called, clinging to the line,
even when their bodies had been taken by a fish.
I can't remember what we caught that day,
only that I never again baited my hooks with frogs,
with those tiny grasping fingers hanging on
as if there were still some hope whatever was
at the end other of the line would save them.

Natural History

The wind keeps shifting through the afternoon,
driving whitecaps to the disappearing shore,
where once, we're told, the sandy beaches lay.
As the lake has risen year after year,
we find our way by absences—islands
now a fringe of weeds above the water-line,
the trees where eagles nested, all blown down.

Quite suddenly, the wind has died, and just
beyond porch screens, a hummingbird returns,
drawn by the vase of flowers on the table.
Once again tonight we'll stay up late
and listen to the cries of loons, thankful
for whatever will remain when we are gone
and all that we have learned of grace.

Fishermen
for Keith
Upper Cormorant Lake, Minnesota

We've finally found the time to get away,
this early June morning with a misty chill
still hanging over the lake. We're alone today,
two bass fishermen, stubbornly working the
thick weed beds along the shore—suddenly
startled by a huge Great Blue rising only
a few yards away from the green walls which
surround us. Such a majestic bird in flight,
so raucous in his scolding cries of departure.

On the slow drive home in fading light
we see the herons flying high above us,
and dream ourselves back to the reeds—
their reeds—where fishermen gather and
it's impossible to know what's coming.

Blues for the Bar Where Everybody Knows Your Name

"Nothing dies as slowly as a scene."
—Richard Hugo

The moose head on the wall is turning white
with dust, the floor tiles cracked and dingy gray,
just like the tin ceilings, where last night's voices
echo still, between the wobbling fans. The
waitresses are waitresses, not servers,
and the glasses are made of glass. Ambiance
is faded signs tacked up at random, mostly
edged with rust. The cute Hamm's bear has
fallen off the wall—at least he found a way
to leave. His shadow's there, right beside
the Marlboro man, who stares into the dark.
The lights are always dim—you'd hate to
see the place if someone ever turned them up.
At least the jukebox knows your favorite tunes,
and rumor has it that they'll get a TV soon.
It could be worse, just like your parents
used to say, and you believed them then, so
why not now? It's cold outside, your food
is mostly warm, and last calls rarely last.
Besides, they're waiting for you at the bar.

Tic-Tat-Too

for Tom Hansen

I'm an old man now and the tattoos I never got
have become scratches, bruises, and tears in
fragile skin I seem to wake up with, wondering
where I've been. They're called Tats now, or
Body Art, and on some people almost every
visible stretch of skin is covered. Maybe
it's to make us guess what might be
lurking underneath their clothing.

People my age have watched their tats turn
into sagging faces, unidentifiable creatures,
or script no longer decipherable. Years ago
there was a woman who saw the face of Jesus
in her breakfast toast and had the whole slice
inked in just above her breast. One has to wonder
what Jesus looks like now—or maybe he's rescued
himself from the large blob he'd one day become.

As a child I loved the ones printed on
thin paper and transferred with a little spit
or water to the backs of hands or skinny arms—
tame stuff, like animals or cartoon characters,
and no kid I knew ever thought to put one on his face
or neck. Years later, it was the ring of barbed wire
around the bicep, but then it spread beyond control,
as if some ancient need for attention was reborn.
Sometimes I've wished I'd had the nerve or arms for
such things, but now I'm satisfied with my bruises,
different each time, and, just like looking at clouds,
whatever I choose to make them.

Father's Day

When I stop for a newspaper
a young Indian man shakes my hand,
wishes me a happy Father's Day, then
asks for a couple of dollars. The bar
next door will be opening soon, and
by the way, I *am* a father, aren't I?
We're old friends by now, and when he
brings up grandkids I have to tell him no.
He stares at me incredulously. I'm 32,
he says, and I've got two. What can I say?
The pity shifts to *his* eyes now, and as I walk
back to my car with my paper I hear him
asking one of his buddies outside the bar
if he can believe a guy as old as me is
without any grandkids, and what's this
bullshit world coming to, anyway?

Perspectives

How unusual to be living a life of continual self-expression,
jotting down little things,
noticing a leaf being carried downstream,
then wondering what will become of me . . .
—Billy Collins

Five miles beneath us is the coast of Labrador,
the pilot announces. We can just make out shoreline—
dark water, darker land, heavy clouds moving in,
and one persistent light, which I can't stop watching.
How I'd like to follow that beam to its distant source,
as my family did with searchlights when I was a child,
on those hot summer nights when we needed
to get out of the apartment for any reason at all.

My mother gave up her place in the front seat to me,
and we shouted directions to my father at the wheel,
a family outing we could afford, even with ice cream
when we finally headed home. I still wonder
why those lights were there and what they were
searching for, though can't remember if I ever asked.

Even if I haven't seen a searchlight in years
nor been over the coast of Labrador again, I have seen
a bright herd of icebergs on another flight, somewhere
high above the North Atlantic. That's what the captain
called them, a herd, and he also mentioned this was
only the second time in all his years of flying he'd seen
so many of them. He couldn't have known that I was
already writing it all down, that I'd been thinking
about the way big things made little by the distance
still qualify as little—like those far-off searchlight beams,
poking tiny holes in the unending dark around us.

Heartland

The winter windchills plunge today,
rekindling survivor's pride—
as if we too are pioneers,
preserving claims at any price.

Prairie grass and clouds are what we have
instead of postcard scenery.
The land, like us, is hard to read,
rewarding only patient eyes.

We've learned to count on better days
to come, the ones we know won't last,
somehow content we'll never find
another place to love like this.

Love Poem
for Betsy

Once, as we were driving home along the Platte
in early March, we stopped, breathless, to watch
as skies filled up with flocks of Sandhill Cranes,
resting here as always on their long flight north—
wave upon wave, their formations blanketing
the stubble fields in precise gray rows—
a kind of love poem, I suppose, and like
all love poems, something to remind us what
we'll never really understand, nor need to.

ACKNOWLEDGMENTS

Most of the poems in this collection were previously published in the following, sometimes in slightly different form, reprinted here with grateful thanks to the editors.

Periodicals

Abraxas, Agassiz Review, Ascent, Ball State University Forum, Chariton Review, Chowder Review, College English, Dacotah Territory, Dakota Arts Quarterly, Deep Breath Online, Everywhere, Flyway, Georgia Review, Gray's Sporting Journal, Great Lakes Review, Great Midwest Review, Great Plains Reader, Great River Review, High Plains Literary Review, Hudson Review, Lake Region Review, The Lamp in the Spine, The Mainstreeter, Midwest Quarterly, Minnesota Folklife Society News, Minnesota Poetry Calendar, North American Review, North Country Anvil, North Dakota Quarterly, Northeast, Northstone Review, Ohio Review, Ottertail Review, Paris Review, Passages North, Pendragon, Platte Valley Review, Poetry Harbor, Poetry Northwest, Poetry Now, Prairie Schooner, Quarterly West, Red Weather, Sidewalks, Research, Ruah, San Marcos Review, South Dakota Review, Sou'wester, Spoon River Quarterly, Tar River Poetry, Thunderbird, Water-Stone Review, West Branch, Zone 3

Anthologies

After the Storm: Poems on the Persian Gulf War; American Life In Poetry; The Anthology of Magazine Verse and Yearbook of American Poetry; As Far as I Can See: Contemporary Writing of the Middle Plains; Beloved on the Earth: 150 Poems of Grief and Gratitude; Beyond Borders: An Anthology of New Writing from Manitoba, Minnesota, Saskatchewan, and the Dakotas; Bringing Gifts; Broad Wings, Long Legs: A Rookery of Heron

Poems; *The Capra Chapbook Anthology; Common Ground: A Gathering of Poems on Rural Life; County Lines: Poems by 130 Minnesota Poets, The Decade Dance: A Celebration of Poems; Don't Forget to Fly; Eating the Pure Light: Homage to Thomas McGrath; Engaging Poetry: Poems That Speak to Us; Farming Words: The Harvest of Literature at a Prairie College; For Sale by Owner; Going over to Your Place: Poems for Each Other; Heartland II: Poets of the Midwest; I Feel a Little Jumpy around You; Imaginative Writing: The Elements of Craft (Third Edition); Kansas City Outloud; Looking for Your Name: A Collection of Contemporary Poems; Midwest Quarterly 50th Anniversary Issue; Minnesota Poetry Outloud; Minnesota Comprehension Assessment; More in Time: A Tribute to Ted Kooser; Naming the World: A Year of Poems and Lessons; A New Geography of Poets; North Dakota Is Everywhere; North Dakota's Literary Heritage; Local News: Poetry about Small Towns; The Passages North Anthology; The Perfect Dragonfly Anthology; The Place My Words Are Looking For; Poetry from A to Z: A Guide for Young Writers; Poets of the Red River; Poetspeak; Prairie Volcano: An Anthology of North Dakota Writing; Pushing the Envelope: Epistolary Poems; Ringing in the Wilderness: Selections from North Country Anvil; River of Time: Fergus Falls 125th Anniversary Anthology; Seeing the Blue Between: Advice and Inspiration for Young Poets; Send My Roots Rain: 52 Weeks of Poetry to Heal Your Grief; South Dakota Review: A Sampler, 1963–83; Strings: A Gathering of Family Poems; Visiting Emily: Poems Inspired by the Life and Work of Emily Dickinson; Visiting Robert: Poems Inspired by the Life and Work of Robert Frost; The Wascana Poetry Anthology; Where One Voice Ends Another Begins: 150 Years of Minnesota Poetry; Wherever Poems Begin: 100 Contemporary Poems; The Windflower Home Almanac of Poetry; Writers and Writing* (Minnesota State University System)

Originally Appeared as Broadsides

"Winter Promises," South Dakota Arts Council, "The Writer Reads" series, 1975

"The Last Time, for Tom McGrath" (with Gaylord Schanilec woodcut), The Rourke Gallery, Moorhead, Minnesota, 1992

"North of North," with Wayne Gudmundson photograph, 1992

"North of North" (revised), Northern Lights Library Network, 2010

"Homesteaders," with Wayne Gudmundson photograph (poster for *Affinities: Collaborations in Poetry and Photography* exhibition), Plains Art Museum, Moorhead, Minnesota, 1993)

"Heartland," with Carl Oltvedt lithograph print, Hannaher Print Studio, Plains Art Museum, Fargo, North Dakota, 2008

Other

"Sins of the Fathers" appeared on *Writer's Almanac*, Minnesota Public Radio

"Absences," " Cautionary Tale," "Center Café," "Driving Through," and "The Way We Said Goodbye" were selected for syndication in *American Life in Poetry*

ALSO BY MARK VINZ

Chapbooks and Other Short Collections

Winter Promises, Bk Mk Press, 1975

Letters to the Poetry Editor, Capra Press, 1975; reprinted in *The Capra Chapbook Anthology*, 1979

Red River Blues, Poetry Texas, 1977

Songs for A Hometown Boy, Solo Press, 1977

Contingency Plans, published as a part of the Autumn 1978 *Ohio Review*

Deep Water, Dakota, Juniper Press, 1980

North of North: A Gathering of Poems, Minnesota State University Moorhead Alumni Foundation, 2007

"Featured Poet" (collection of poems with essay, "The Habit of Poetry"), *Great River Review*, vol. 7, no. 1 (1986), pp. 25–45

"A Vinz Poetry Sampler, 1972–87," in *Stirring the Deep: The Poetry of Mark Vinz*, by Thom Tammaro, Spoon River Poetry Press, 1989, pp. 63–99

In Harm's Way: Poems of Childhood (with Clarence Wolfshohl), El Grito del Lobo, 2013

Books of Poems

Climbing the Stairs, Spoon River Poetry Press, 1983

Mixed Blessings, Spoon River Poetry Press, 1989

Minnesota Gothic (with Wayne Gudmundson photographs), Milkweed Editions, 1992

Affinities (with Wayne Gudmundson photographs), Dacotah Territory Press, 1998

Long Distance, Midwest Writers Publishing House, 2005

The Work Is All, Red Dragonfly Editions, 2011

Permanent Record, Red Dragonfly Editions, 2015

Other Books

The Weird Kid (prose poems), New Rivers Press, 1983
Late Night Calls: Prose Poems and Short Fiction, New Rivers
    Press, 1992
Man of the House: Scenes from a '50s Childhood (memoir), New
    Rivers Press, 2018

ABOUT THE AUTHOR

Mark Vinz was born in Rugby, North Dakota, grew up in Minneapolis and the Kansas City area, and attended the universities of Kansas (BA in English 1964, MA in English, 1966) and New Mexico (two additional years of graduate study in English). He is now Professor Emeritus at Minnesota State University Moorhead, where he taught in the English department for thirty-nine years and also served as the first (1995–1998) coordinator of MSUM's Master of Fine Arts in Creative Writing program. His poems, prose poems, stories, and essays have appeared in over two hundred magazines and anthologies and several book-length collections.

Mark is the recipient of a National Endowment for the Arts poetry fellowship, six Pen Syndicated Fiction Awards, three Minnesota Book Awards, the Milkweed Editions Seeing Double Competition (with Wayne Gudmundson), and the New Rivers Press Minnesota Voices competition. He is also co-editor of several anthologies, including *Inheriting the Land: Contemporary Voices from the Midwest* (with Thom Tammaro, University of Minnesota Press) and *The Party Train: A Collection of North American Prose Poetry* (with Robert Alexander and C. W. Truesdale, New Rivers Press). From 1971–1981, he was the editor of the poetry journal *Dacotah Territory* and also Dacotah Territory Press, from 1973–2007, producing over fifty chapbooks of poetry by writers from the region. He has done extensive work with K-12 students in both the North Dakota and Minnesota Writers in the Schools programs and has given poetry and jazz performances throughout the region with pianist David Ferreira and bassist Bill Law and Jeremy Cahill.

He was the co-founder with Joe Richardson and president of Plains Distribution Service, Inc., a non-profit distributor of small press books and magazines by Midwestern authors and presses (1975–1981). The Plains Bookbus, a kind of traveling bookstore, visited schools and libraries throughout the Upper Midwest, also sponsoring over three hundred readings, lectures, and workshops in the late 1970s.

Affinities, a gallery show of poetry and photography with Wayne Gudmundson, appeared at Plains Art Museum in the 1990s, as well as at several sites in North Dakota and the House Office Building in Washington D.C.

In 2014, he was honored with the Kay Sexton Award, which is presented to an individual or organization in recognition of long-standing dedication and outstanding work in fostering books, reading, and literary activity in Minnesota.

Mark and his wife, Betsy, now live in Fargo, North Dakota. They are the parents of two adult daughters, Katie and Sarah.

ABOUT THE PRESS

North Dakota State University Press (NDSU Press) exists to stimulate and coordinate interdisciplinary regional scholarship. These regions include the Red River Valley, the state of North Dakota, the plains of North America (comprising both the Great Plains of the United States and the prairies of Canada), and comparable regions of other continents. We publish peer reviewed regional scholarship shaped by national and international events and comparative studies.

Neither topic nor discipline limits the scope of NDSU Press publications. We consider manuscripts in any field of learning. We define our scope, however, by a regional focus in accord with the press's mission. Generally, works published by NDSU Press address regional life directly, as the subject of study. Such works contribute to scholarly knowledge of region (that is, discovery of new knowledge) or to public consciousness of region (that is, dissemination of information, or interpretation of regional experience). Where regions abroad are treated, either for comparison or because of ties to those North American regions of primary concern to the press, the linkages are made plain. For nearly three-quarters of a century, NDSU Press has published substantial trade books, but the line of publications is not limited to that genre. We also publish textbooks (at any level), reference books, anthologies, reprints, papers, proceedings, and monographs. The press also considers works of poetry or fiction, provided they are established regional classics or they promise to assume landmark or reference status for the region. We select biographical or autobiographical works carefully for their prospective contribution to regional knowledge and culture. All publications, in whatever genre, are of such quality and substance as to embellish the imprint of NDSU Press.

We changed our imprint to North Dakota State University Press in January 2016. Prior to that, and since 1950, we published as the North Dakota Institute for Regional Studies Press. We continue to operate under the umbrella of the North Dakota Institute for Regional Studies, located at North Dakota State University.